Contents

Summary

To provide information about its plans beyond the coming year, the Department of Defense (DoD) generally develops a five-year plan, called the Future Years Defense Program (FYDP), that is associated with the budget it submits to the Congress. Because decisions made in the near term can have consequences for the defense budget in the longer term, the Congressional Budget Office (CBO) regularly examines DoD's FYDP and projects its budgetary impact for roughly a decade beyond the period it covers. For this analysis, CBO used the FYDP that was provided to the Congress in April 2014; it spans fiscal years 2015 to 2019, and CBO's projections span the years 2015 to 2030.

For fiscal year 2015, DoD requested appropriations totaling $555 billion. Of that amount, $496 billion is for the base budget and $59 billion is for what are termed overseas contingency operations (OCO). The base budget covers programs that constitute the department's normal activities, such as the development and procurement of weapon systems and the day-to-day operations of the military and civilian workforce. Funding for OCO pays for U.S. involvement in the war in Afghanistan and other nonroutine military activities elsewhere. The FYDP describes DoD's plans for its normal activities and therefore generally corresponds to the base budget.

DoD's 2015 plans differ from its 2014 plans in important ways. For example, in an effort to reduce costs, the current FYDP includes sizable cuts in the number of military personnel, particularly in the Army.

CBO produced two projections of the base-budget costs of DoD's plans as reflected in the FYDP and other long-term planning documents released by DoD. The "CBO projection" uses CBO's estimates of the costs of military activities and the extent to which those costs will change over time; those estimates reflect DoD's historical experience. The "FYDP and extension" starts with DoD's estimates of the costs of its plans through 2019 and extends them beyond 2019 using DoD's estimates if available and CBO's projections of price and compensation trends for the overall economy if DoD's estimates are not available. Neither projection should be viewed as a prediction of future funding for DoD's activities; rather, the projections are estimates of the costs of executing the department's current plans without changes.

The amount requested for the base budget in 2015 would comply with the limits on budget authority established by the Budget Control Act of 2011 as subsequently modified, hereafter referred to simply as the Budget Control Act (BCA). After 2015, however, the costs of DoD's plans under both projections would significantly exceed CBO's estimate of the funding the department would receive under the BCA, which limits appropriations for national defense through 2021. To remain in compliance with the BCA after 2015, DoD would have to make sharp additional cuts to the size of its forces, curtail the development and purchase of weapons, reduce the extent of its operations and training, or implement some combination of those three actions.

The Inflation-Adjusted Costs of DoD's Plans Would Increase by 1.2 Percent per Year Through 2030 Under the CBO Projection

The costs to implement DoD's 2015 plans would increase over the next 15 years in real terms (that is, after adjusting to remove the effects of inflation). Under the CBO projection, the real cost of the plans would start at $497 billion in 2015, jump to $533 billion in 2016, and continue growing thereafter, reaching $541 billion in 2019 and $598 billion in 2030 (see Summary Figure 1). The average annual growth rate of the cost from 2015 to 2030 would be 1.2 percent, resulting in a 20 percent

Summary Figure 1.

Costs of DoD's Plans

Billions of 2015 Dollars

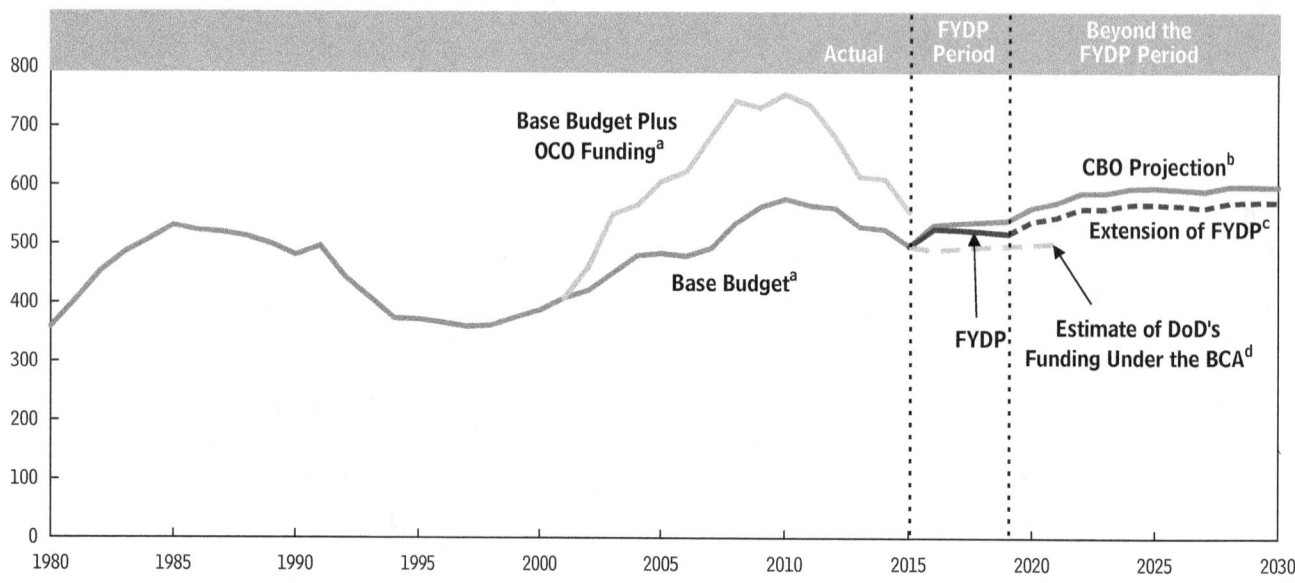

Source: Congressional Budget Office.

Note: DoD = Department of Defense; OCO = overseas contingency operations; FYDP = Future Years Defense Program; FYDP period = 2015 through 2019, the period for which DoD's plans are fully specified; BCA = Budget Control Act of 2011 as modified by the Bipartisan Budget Act of 2013.

a.   Base-budget data include supplemental and emergency funding before 2002. For 2002 to 2015, supplemental and emergency funding for overseas contingency operations, such as those in Afghanistan and Iraq, and for other purposes is shown separately from the base-budget data. No OCO funding is shown for 2016 and later.

b.   The CBO projection of the base budget incorporates costs that are consistent with DoD's historical experience.

c.   For the extension of the FYDP from 2020 to 2030, CBO projects the costs of DoD's plans using the department's estimates of costs to the extent they are available and costs that are consistent with CBO's projections of price and compensation trends in the overall economy when the department's estimates are not available.

d.   The estimate assumes that DoD would receive 95.5 percent of the BCA's funding limit for national defense, which corresponds to DoD's average share of that funding in base budgets since 2001.

increase over the next decade and a half. CBO projects that the two largest parts of DoD's budget would increase by different amounts and with very different profiles over that period:

■ Operation and support (O&S)—which includes compensation for the department's military and civilian employees, military health care, and various other operation and maintenance activities—accounts for about two-thirds of the cost to implement DoD's plans in 2015. CBO projects that those costs would rise fairly steadily between 2015 and 2030, with average growth of 1.1 percent a year in real terms and cumulative growth of 18 percent. That growth would occur despite a 6 percent decrease in the size of the military.

■ Acquisition—which includes research, development, test, and evaluation as well as procurement of weapon systems, munitions, and other equipment—accounts for about one-third of the cost to implement DoD's plans in 2015. CBO projects that those costs would jump by 42 percent in real terms between 2015 and 2022 but then trend downward through 2030. Costs in 2030 would be 22 percent higher than in 2015.

According to the CBO projection, the average real cost of DoD's base-budget plans from 2015 through 2019 would exceed average spending for DoD from 1980 to 2014 by $64 billion a year. Moreover, the average real cost of DoD's plans from 2015 through 2030 would exceed the 1980–2014 average by $105 billion a year.

The growth in DoD's costs under the CBO projection of the base budget would be somewhat less than CBO's projection of the growth of the U.S. economy. Consequently, DoD's costs as a share of gross domestic product (GDP) would decrease slowly over most of the projection period, from 2.8 percent of GDP in 2015 to 2.5 percent in 2025 and 2.3 percent in 2030.

The Inflation-Adjusted Costs of DoD's Plans Would Increase by 1.0 Percent per Year Through 2030 Under the FYDP and Extension

For most categories of DoD's budget, costs under the CBO projection are higher than the costs estimated by DoD in the FYDP and the extrapolated costs for the extension of the FYDP. In particular, the growth reflected in the CBO projection for military pay, the costs of developing and buying weapons, and the costs of providing health care is higher than the growth incorporated by DoD in the FYDP and extrapolated by CBO for the FYDP extension:

■ Using DoD's estimates of costs and CBO's extension of those estimates, the real cost of DoD's plans would grow at an average annual rate of 1.0 percent between 2015 and 2030, or 0.2 percentage points more slowly than under the CBO projection.

■ Real O&S costs would rise by 1.0 percent a year, on average, during that period, or 0.1 percentage point more slowly than under the CBO projection.

■ Real costs for acquisition would increase by 32 percent between 2015 and 2022, 10 percentage points less than under the CBO projection. As in the CBO projection, those costs would decline between 2022 and 2030.

The Costs of DoD's Plans Would Significantly Exceed the Limits Established by the Budget Control Act

Although DoD has scaled back its plans since last year, CBO estimates that the cost of those plans after 2015 would still significantly exceed the funding that would be

provided to the department under the BCA, which limits discretionary appropriations through 2021. If DoD continues to receive its historical share of the national defense budget, CBO's analysis yields three conclusions:[1]

■ Under the CBO projection, the cumulative cost of DoD's base-budget plans for 2015 through 2021 would be higher in nominal terms by $332 billion, or about $47 billion a year, than the funding that would be provided to DoD under the limits set by the BCA. The gap would be $308 billion after adjusting for inflation.

■ Under the FYDP and extension, the cumulative cost of DoD's base-budget plans for 2015 through 2021 would be higher in nominal terms by $215 billion, or about $31 billion a year, than the funding that would be provided under the BCA. The gap would be $200 billion after adjusting for inflation.

■ Under either projection, the costs of DoD's plans in the 2015 FYDP would be closer to the limits established by the BCA than would the costs of the plans in the 2014 FYDP. For example, between 2015 and 2021, the gap between the BCA's limits and CBO's projection for the 2015 plan is about half as large as the gap computed from CBO's projection for the 2014 plan.

In any year for which discretionary appropriations are subject to the BCA, if the Congress appropriates more for DoD's base budget than the amount permitted under the law, the difference between the appropriated amount and the BCA limit would be subject to sequestration (the cancellation of budgetary resources after they have been appropriated).

---

1. The Budget Control Act limits discretionary budget authority for national defense (budget function 050) rather than for the DoD component of national defense (budget subfunction 051). Since 2001, DoD has received an average of 95.5 percent of the budget authority for national defense, excluding OCO; the remaining 4.5 percent has gone to nuclear weapons activities of the Department of Energy and the national security activities of other agencies. CBO estimated DoD's future share of national defense funding under the BCA's limits by assuming that the department would continue to receive that historical share.

Projections of the Costs of DoD's Plans

Fiscal pressures on the federal government have prompted increased scrutiny of the Department of Defense's (DoD's) budget. Although funding decisions are usually made on an annual basis, near-term decisions about issues such as pay raises, health benefits for military retirees, and the acquisition of weapon systems can have effects on the composition and costs of the nation's armed forces that last many years.

To provide information about its plans beyond the coming year, DoD usually issues a Future Years Defense Program (FYDP) in conjunction with its annual budget request. The FYDP is a detailed description of DoD's plans and DoD's estimate of the costs of those plans over the next five years. The latest FYDP, which was released in April 2014, covers fiscal years 2015 to 2019.

DoD also publishes information about its plans beyond the FYDP period for some activities, such as shipbuilding and aircraft procurement. The Congressional Budget Office (CBO) uses that information, as well as its extrapolations of the plans contained in the FYDP for other activities, to project the costs of DoD's plans beyond the FYDP period. This study presents those projections through 2030.

DoD's Budget Request for 2015

The Administration's proposals for funding DoD in 2015 can be separated into three parts:[1]

- A $496 billion request for the base budget, which funds the normal activities of the department, including manning and training the force, developing and procuring weapon systems, and running the day-to-day operations of the military and civilian workforce;

- A $59 billion request for overseas contingency operations (OCO), which include the war in Afghanistan and other nonroutine military activities elsewhere; and

- A proposal for an additional $26 billion as part of the Opportunity, Growth, and Security Initiative (OGSI), which would be offset with a package of increased revenues and cuts to mandatory programs elsewhere in the federal budget.

CBO's analysis focuses on the first part of the request, DoD's base budget. Although OCO funding has accounted for a significant fraction of DoD's total spending over the past 12 years, future spending for such operations will depend on how conditions evolve in Afghanistan, Iraq, Syria, and elsewhere. The OGSI, which is discussed later in this chapter, is not part of DoD's request for its base budget but is essentially a "wish list" of items for consideration by the Congress.

The request for DoD's base budget in 2015 is, after accounting for inflation, 2 percent less than the amount that the Congress appropriated for 2014. If DoD continued to receive its historical share of the national defense budget, its request for fiscal year 2015 would be consistent with the 2015 limit on discretionary funding for national defense that was established under the Budget Control Act of 2011 as modified by the Bipartisan Budget Act of 2013, hereafter referred to simply as the BCA. (Indeed, 2015 is the first year for which DoD's request has stayed within the limits of the BCA.) For

---

1. The funding for DoD can be expressed in several ways. In this analysis, CBO used total obligational authority (TOA) because the FYDP is presented in terms of TOA. Discretionary budget authority, which CBO focuses on in other contexts, usually differs only slightly from TOA in the budget year and is almost identical to TOA in the years beyond the budget year. For example, DoD's tally of its base-budget request for 2015 was $495.6 billion in discretionary budget authority and $496.4 billion in TOA.

Figure 1-1.

Costs of DoD's Plans, by Appropriation Category

Billions of 2015 Dollars

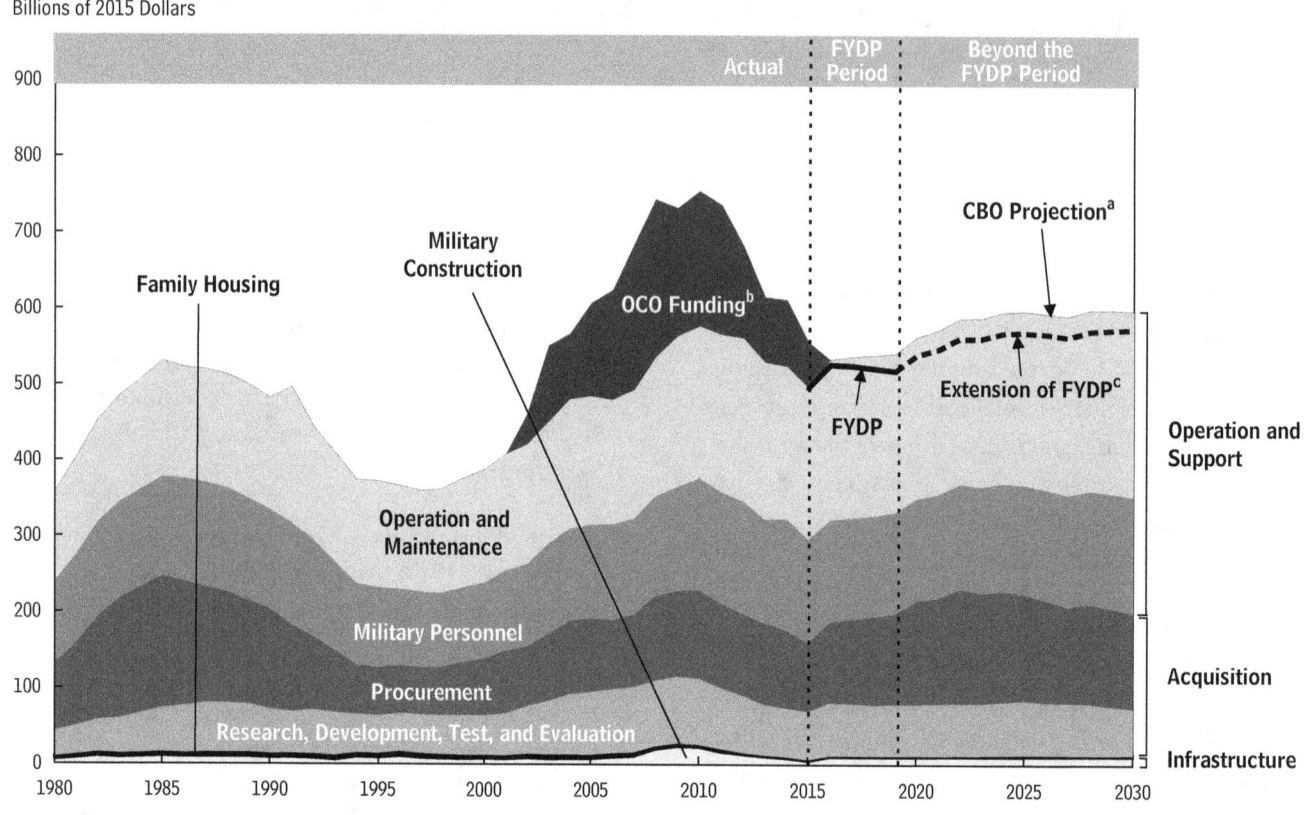

Source: Congressional Budget Office.

Notes: The amounts shown for the Future Years Defense Program (FYDP) and the extension of the FYDP are totals for all categories.

DoD = Department of Defense; OCO = overseas contingency operations; FYDP period = 2015 through 2019, the period for which DoD's plans are fully specified.

a.   Each category shows the CBO projection of the base budget from 2015 to 2030. That projection incorporates costs that are consistent with DoD's historical experience.

b.   Base-budget data include supplemental and emergency funding before 2002. For 2002 to 2015, supplemental and emergency funding for overseas contingency operations, such as those in Afghanistan and Iraq, and for other purposes is shown separately from the base-budget data. No OCO funding is shown for 2016 and later.

c.   For the extension of the FYDP from 2020 to 2030, CBO projects the costs of DoD's plans using the department's estimates of costs to the extent they are available and costs that are consistent with CBO's projections of price and compensation trends in the overall economy when the department's estimates are not available.

2016 through 2019, however, DoD's plans would cost significantly more than the department would receive under the current BCA limits. The implications of the BCA for DoD's funding are discussed later in this chapter.

Nearly all of DoD's funding for its base budget is provided in six appropriation categories (see Figure 1-1). CBO organized those six categories into three broader groups: operation and support (O&S), acquisition, and infrastructure.

Operation and support includes appropriations for operation and maintenance (O&M) and for military personnel. O&M appropriations fund most of the day-to-day operations of the military, the maintenance of equipment, the purchase of spare parts, the training of military units, the majority of costs of the military's health care program, compensation for most of DoD's civilian employees, and payments to DoD's support contractors.[2] Military personnel appropriations fund compensation for uniformed service members, including pay, housing and food allowances, and related items, such as moving service members and their families to new duty stations. O&M represents the largest portion—about 40 percent—of the request for the base budget in 2015, followed by military personnel at 27 percent.

Acquisition includes appropriations for procurement and research, development, test, and evaluation (RDT&E). Procurement appropriations fund the purchase of new weapon systems, munitions, and other equipment as well as upgrades to existing weapon systems. RDT&E appropriations pay for the development of technology and weapons. Procurement represents 18 percent of the request for the base budget in 2015, and RDT&E represents 13 percent.

Infrastructure refers to construction at DoD's facilities as well as activities associated with DoD's military family housing. Appropriations for military construction and family housing make up less than 2 percent of the request for the base budget in 2015.

CBO's Approach for the Projections

This report provides CBO's independent projections of the costs of implementing DoD's plans for operation and support, acquisition, and infrastructure contained in the 2015 FYDP. Going beyond the 2015–2019 period covered by those plans, CBO projects costs through 2030. In making its projections, CBO relied on the number of military personnel, acquisition plans, and policies reflected in the 2015 FYDP as well as the long-term acquisition plans that DoD publishes in Selected Acquisition Reports and other official documents, such as the Navy's 30-year shipbuilding plan and DoD's 30-year aviation plan.[3] For the years beyond 2019, CBO assumed that the force structure and number of military and civilian personnel would remain at the levels planned for 2019.

CBO made two projections of the costs of DoD's plans for 2015 through 2030:

■ The *CBO projection*, which is based on CBO's estimates of future costs, and

■ The *FYDP and extension*, which is based on DoD's FYDP through 2019, DoD's estimates of costs beyond 2019 if they were available, and CBO's projections of price and compensation trends for the overall economy if DoD's estimates were not available.

For the CBO projection covering 2015 to 2019, CBO used DoD's estimates of costs unless those estimates differed significantly from historical experience—as they do for military pay, health care, acquisition, and military construction, in which case the historical experience was used instead. For example, the CBO projection does not include savings that would accrue from proposals in the FYDP to increase the amount that military service members and retirees would pay for DoD-provided health care because the Congress has resisted such proposals in the past. (Because of the differences between DoD's estimates and historical experience, the CBO projection for the base budget in 2015 is $840 million higher than DoD's request.) For 2020 to 2030, the CBO projection incorporates CBO's forecasts of growth in some costs (such as for pay and health care in the armed forces) and CBO's estimates of DoD's other costs (such as for acquisition, infrastructure, and some parts of operation and maintenance) based on historical experience (see Table 1-1 for details).

For the FYDP and extension, CBO used DoD's estimates of costs in the FYDP for 2015 through 2019. For 2020 through 2030, CBO projected the costs of DoD's plans using the department's estimates of longer-term costs if they were available (for some major weapon systems, for instance) and costs that were consistent with CBO's outlook for the economy as a whole if estimates by the department were not available (for example, for pay; see Table 1-1).

---

2. For this analysis, CBO folded the amounts appropriated for most revolving funds, such as the one for the Defense Commissary Agency, into the appropriation for operation and maintenance. The exception is amounts in the National Defense Sealift Fund that were used to purchase ships prior to 2015, which CBO treated as acquisition. Appropriations in the base budget for revolving funds have averaged less than $3 billion per year since 1980.

3. If a weapon system reaches the end of its service life before 2030 and DoD has not planned a replacement system, CBO assumes that the department will develop and purchase a new system to replace the aging one. DoD has not published plans for minor procurement programs extending beyond the FYDP period. Therefore, CBO estimated costs for those programs on the basis of historical correlations between funding for major and minor programs.

Table 1-1.

Methodology Used in CBO's Two Projections of the Costs of DoD's Plans

	CBO Projection	FYDP and Extension
Military Pay	DoD's estimate in 2015; rate of growth matches ECI after 2015	DoD's estimates through 2019; rate of growth matches ECI after 2019
Civilian Pay	DoD's estimates through 2019; rate of growth matches ECI after 2019	Same as CBO projection
Military Health Care	DoD's estimates through 2019, excluding savings from cost-sharing proposals that the Congress has historically rejected; after 2019, tracks CBO's projection of growth rates for health care spending nationally	DoD's estimates through 2019; after 2019, tracks CBO's projection of growth rates for health care spending nationally
Operation and Maintenance[a]	DoD's estimates through 2019; after 2019, costs aside from pay and military health care grow at the historical average rate	Same as CBO projection
Acquisition	DoD's estimates with historical average cost growth	DoD's estimates with no cost growth
Military Construction	DoD's estimate in 2015; in 2016, costs equal 1/67 of the total replacement cost of DoD's facilities and, thereafter, grow at CBO's projection of the growth rate for construction costs nationally	DoD's estimates through 2019; in 2020, costs equal the historical average and, thereafter, grow at CBO's projection of the growth rate for construction costs nationally
Family Housing	DoD's estimates through 2019; after 2019, costs grow with inflation	Same as CBO projection

Source: Congressional Budget Office.

Note: DoD = Department of Defense; FYDP = Future Years Defense Program; ECI = employment cost index for wages and salaries in the private sector, as reported by the Bureau of Labor Statistics.

a.   Operation and maintenance costs excluding civilian pay and military health care.

For several categories of DoD's plans, costs in the CBO projection are higher than the costs estimated by DoD in the FYDP and extrapolated by CBO in the extension of the FYDP. In particular, during the past several decades, the costs of developing and buying weapons have been, on average, 20 percent to 30 percent higher than the department's initial published estimates. DoD and the Congress have made some changes to the way that weapon systems are developed and purchased, but it is not yet clear whether those efforts will lower the growth in costs below the historical experience.

The two projections are not predictions of future funding for DoD; rather, they are estimates of the costs of executing the department's current plans. Defense plans can be affected by unpredicted changes in the international security environment, decisions made by the Congress, and other factors that could result in substantial departures from the department's current intentions. One such factor is that DoD and the Congress frequently respond to higher-than-expected costs of weapon systems by changing acquisition plans—for example, by delaying or reducing purchases of weapon systems or canceling systems outright. Another increasingly prominent factor is the pressure on the federal budget as a whole. Except for fiscal year 2015, the Budget Control Act limits DoD's funding to amounts that are below the costs of implementing the department's plans, according to both CBO's and DoD's estimates.

Projections of Costs

CBO's projections include the costs of DoD's base-budget plans over two time spans: the period from 2015 to 2019, which is covered by the FYDP, and the period from 2020 to 2030.

Table 1-2.

Comparison of the CBO Projection of DoD's Future Years Defense Program and DoD's Projection

Billions of 2015 Dollars

	2014	Budget Request, 2015	2016	2017	2018	2019	Total, 2015- 2019
				FYDP Period			
CBO Projection, Base Budget	525	497	533	536	539	541	2,646
DoD's 2015 FYDP, Base Budget	525	496	526	525	521	518	2,586
Difference Between the CBO Projection and DoD's FYDP	0	1	7	12	17	23	60

Source: Congressional Budget Ofice.

Notes: The CBO projection incorporates costs that are consistent with the Department of Defense's (DoD's) historical experience.

FYDP = Future Years Defense Program; FYDP period = 2015 through 2019, the period for which DoD's plans are fully specified.

Costs of DoD's Plans During the FYDP Period (2015 to 2019)

According to the CBO projection, the annual cost of carrying out DoD's plans would rise sharply from $497 billion in 2015 to $533 billion in 2016 and then more slowly to $541 billion in real (inflation-adjusted) terms by 2019 (see Table 1-2). DoD's estimates in the FYDP also anticipate a sharp increase in cost in 2016 followed by a slight decrease (in real terms) through 2019, with an average annual cost of $523 billion during those years.

Cumulative costs for 2015 through 2019 under the CBO projection are about $2.6 trillion, some 2 percent greater than the cumulative costs under DoD's estimates. Most of that difference results from CBO's higher estimates of the cost to pay military personnel, develop and procure new weapon systems, and provide health care to service members and retirees and their families.

Costs of DoD's Plans Beyond the FYDP Period (2020 through 2030)

According to the CBO projection, the annual cost (in 2015 dollars) of carrying out DoD's plans would rise from $541 billion in 2019 to $596 billion in 2024 and remain at about that level through 2030 (see Table 1-3). Between 2019 and 2030, the average real increase in costs would be 1.0 percent per year. That increase can be explained by rising costs of operation and maintenance and of pay and benefits for military service members and retirees; costs for procurement would grow rapidly

through 2022 but then decline nearly to the 2019 amount by 2030 (see Figure 1-2).

Real costs for O&M are projected to grow by an average of 1.4 percent per year, from $209 billion in 2019 to $245 billion in 2030. That growth would result from the rising costs of medical care for military personnel and their families, pay and benefits for civilian workers, and maintaining equipment. Costs for military personnel would increase by an average of 1.3 percent per year, from $133 billion in 2019 to $153 billion in 2030 (in 2015 dollars), reflecting pay raises that are projected to exceed the economywide rate of inflation.

The real costs of procuring weapon systems are projected to increase sharply between 2015 and 2022 and then decline slowly thereafter. The real costs of conducting research, development, testing, and evaluation of weapon systems are projected to edge up through the mid-2020s and then decline slightly. Taking those costs together, the real cost of acquisition would peak at $220 billion in 2022 under the CBO projection. That cost would gradually diminish thereafter, to $187 billion in 2030. In those later years, the department would have largely completed its current modernization programs. DoD has not, however, articulated plans for all of the modernization programs that might be needed toward the end of CBO's projection period. Although CBO's analysis includes several such programs, the projected decline might not occur if DoD's modernization goals for the 2020s are more extensive than those reflected in CBO's projections.

Table 1-3.

Historical Costs and the CBO Projection of Costs of DoD's Plans in Selected Years

Billions of 2015 Dollars

	2001	2012	FYDP Period 2015	FYDP Period 2019	Beyond the FYDP Period 2024	Beyond the FYDP Period 2030	Average, 2015–2030
			Base Budget				
Operation and Support							
Operation and maintenance[a]	153	215	200	209	225	245	222
Military personnel	105	148	136	133	142	153	141
Subtotal	258	363	336	342	367	398	363
Acquisition							
Procurement	83	107	91	120	146	126	128
Research, development, test, and evaluation	55	75	64	68	71	62	68
Subtotal	138	183	154	187	217	187	196
Infrastructure							
Military construction	7	13	5	10	11	11	10
Family housing	5	2	1	1	1	1	1
Subtotal	12	15	7	12	12	13	12
Total Base Budget	408	562	497	541	596	598	571
			Supplemental and Emergency Funding for Overseas Contingency Operations				
Total OCO Funding	n.a.	121	59	n.a. [b]	n.a. [b]	n.a. [b]	n.a. [b]
			Total				
Total DoD Budget	408	682	556	n.a. [b]	n.a. [b]	n.a. [b]	n.a. [b]

Source: Congressional Budget Office.

Notes: The CBO projection incorporates costs that are consistent with the Department of Defense's (DoD's) historical experience.

FYDP = Future Years Defense Program; FYDP period = 2015 through 2019, the period for which DoD's plans are fully specified; OCO = overseas contingency operations; n.a. = not applicable.

a.   For this analysis, CBO folded appropriations for most revolving funds (such as the one for the Defense Commissary Agency) into the appropriations for operation and maintenance.

b.   DoD did not request OCO funding beyond 2015, and CBO did not project it.

The costs of DoD's plans would be lower than the CBO projection if the Congress adopts DoD's proposals to increase cost sharing for users of the Military Health System and to raise pay for military personnel more slowly between 2015 and 2019 than is specified in current law, and if DoD is able to rein in the growth in the costs of weapon systems or operations. Projected costs under the FYDP and extension, which incorporates those alternative policies and assumptions, would be about $573 billion in 2030—about $25 billion, or 4 percent, less than the amount in the CBO projection.

Costs of DoD's Plans in the Context of the Budget Control Act

The Budget Control Act of 2011 established limits (caps) on most discretionary appropriations for national defense through 2021. The limits imposed by the BCA have been modified twice, first by the American Taxpayer Relief Act of 2012 and more recently by the Bipartisan Budget Act of 2013 (see Box 1-1). Taken together, those acts eased the constraints on funding from 2013 to 2015 but left intact the limits imposed by the BCA for the remaining years.

Figure 1-2.

CBO Projection of Base-Budget Costs of DoD's Plans, by Appropriation Category

Billions of 2015 Dollars

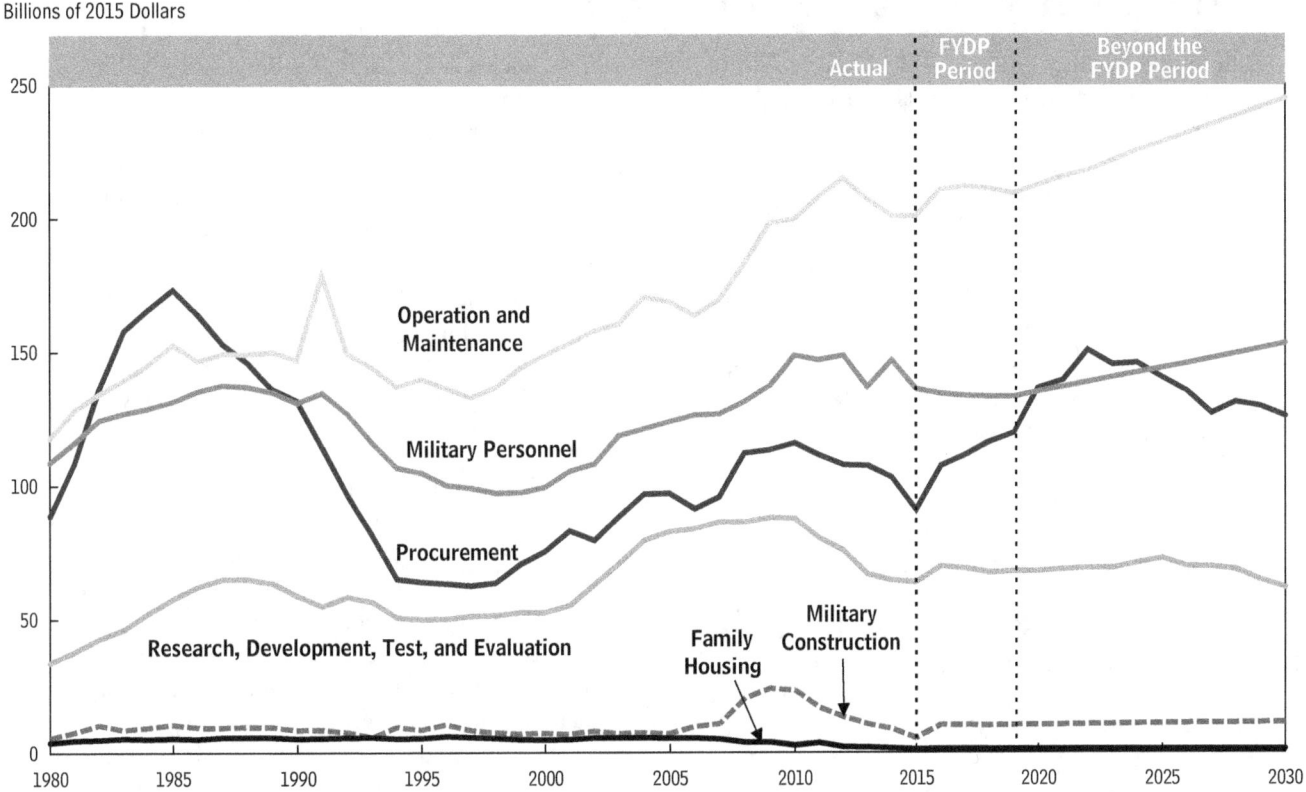

Source: Congressional Budget Office.

Notes: Base-budget data include supplemental and emergency funding before 2002.

DoD = Department of Defense; FYDP = Future Years Defense Program; FYDP period = 2015 through 2019, the period for which DoD's plans are fully specified.

The Administration's request for DoD in 2015 complies with the BCA's cap for the year. At $496 billion, it is 95.2 percent of the $521 billion cap for national defense, a level similar to the 95.5 percent share of national defense funding that DoD has received, on average, since 2001. However, if national defense funding equals the BCA's caps from 2016 through 2021 and DoD receives 95.5 percent of that funding, DoD's budgets would be significantly lower than the costs of DoD's current plans:

- In that scenario, DoD's funding would be $182 billion ($173 billion in constant dollars) less than DoD's costs under the CBO projection for 2015 through 2019 (see Table 1-4). For 2020 and 2021, DoD's funding would fall short of DoD's costs under the CBO projection by an additional $150 billion ($135 billion in constant dollars).

- In that scenario, DoD's funding would be $119 billion ($114 billion in constant dollars) less than DoD's costs under the FYDP for 2015 through 2019, and an additional $96 billion ($86 billion in constant dollars) less than the costs under the extension of the FYDP in 2020 and 2021.[4]

The accrual of such large differences in just two years beyond the FYDP period illustrates the sharp increase in costs for DoD's plans seen in both projections after 2019 (see Summary Figure 1 on page 2).

---

4. According to DoD's estimates, the cost of its budget plans will exceed its share of the funding under the caps established in the BCA by $115 billion in nominal terms from 2016 through 2019. That total is slightly lower than CBO's estimate of $119 billion because DoD assumes that it will receive a slightly higher share of national defense funding in those years.

Box 1-1.

The Budget Control Act of 2011 and DoD's Budget

The Budget Control Act of 2011 (BCA) set limits (caps) on discretionary appropriations through 2021 and included automatic enforcement procedures that took effect because lawmakers failed to enact additional deficit reduction legislation by January 15, 2012. Once triggered, those automatic enforcement procedures had two effects. First, they imposed sequestration (a cancellation of budgetary resources) for 2013 and also reduced the funding that was to be allowed each year from 2014 to 2021 to amounts that were below those initial caps. Second, they allocated the overall limits on funding for the 2014–2021 period between national defense and nondefense budget functions by setting separate caps for each. The limits imposed by the BCA have been modified twice, first by the American Taxpayer Relief Act of 2012 and more recently by the Bipartisan Budget Act of 2013. Taken together, those acts eased the constraints on the funding for discretionary programs from 2013 to 2015 but left intact the limits imposed by the BCA for the remaining years. [1]

In the BCA, defense appropriations are defined as appropriations for budget function 050 (national defense). That category includes the Department of Defense's (DoD's) military activities, the nuclear weapons activities of the Department of Energy (DOE), and the national security activities of several other agencies. Since 2001, funding for DoD has accounted for, on average, 95.5 percent of total funding for budget function 050, excluding funding for overseas contingency operations. In each of those years, DoD's share of national defense funding has been within 0.5 percentage points of that average. For the purpose of estimating the BCA's limits for DoD alone, the Congressional Budget Office (CBO) assumed that the department would be allocated the same share of total discretionary funding for national defense that would be allowed under the BCA's limits.

For 2015, the Administration has requested discretionary funding of $496 billion for DoD's base budget (budget subfunction 051); about $18 billion for atomic energy defense activities, primarily within DOE (budget subfunction 053); and about $35 billion for other defense-related activities (budget subfunction 054). Of that $35 billion, $8 billion is for activities normally funded in that category (for example, some national security operations of the Federal Bureau of Investigation) and $28 billion is for the Administration's Opportunity, Growth, and Security Initiative (OGSI). The OGSI includes $56 billion in discretionary funding beyond that in the rest of the Administration's budget request, with that amount split equally between national security and other programs and packaged with offsetting cuts to mandatory spending and increases in revenues.

Leaving aside the $28 billion for the OGSI, the Administration's request for funding for national security complies with the BCA's limits for 2015, and DoD's portion of that funding—95.2 percent—is consistent with past experience. Although $26 billion of the OGSI would fund DoD programs, CBO did not treat that amount as part of DoD's base-budget request.

---

1.   The American Taxpayer Relief Act of 2012 (ATRA) lowered the amount to be sequestered in 2013—from discretionary programs—by $24 billion (split evenly between defense and nondefense programs), which effectively increased funding levels for that year. For 2014, ATRA and the Bipartisan Budget Act of 2013 combined to raise the defense and nondefense caps by about $18 billion each; for 2015, they combined to raise the caps by about $9 billion each. See Congressional Budget Office, *The Budget and Economic Outlook: 2014 to 2024* (February 2014), Box 1-1, www.cbo.gov/publication/45010.

Although the 2015 FYDP calls for budgets that would exceed the BCA's limits after 2015, the total difference between the CBO projection and the BCA's limits for 2015 through 2021 is only about half the difference estimated by CBO in its analysis of the 2014 FYDP. Much of that reduction was achieved by cutting the planned size of the military force. Under last year's plan, the active-duty force was slated to drop from 1.40 million personnel in 2013 to 1.33 million by 2018; under this year's plan, the force would decrease to 1.24 million by 2018. Specific elements of the services' force structures would also be eliminated. For example, refueling and overhauling

Table 1-4.

Costs of DoD's Plans and DoD's Funding Projected Under the Budget Control Act of 2011

Billions of Dollars

	FYDP Period					2020	2021	Totals	
								2015-2019	2015-2021
	2015	2016	2017	2018	2019	2020	2021	2015-2019	2015-2021
Nominal Dollars									
CBO Projection[a]	497	542	556	570	584	620	642	2,749	4,011
FYDP and Extension[b]	496	535	544	551	559	594	614	2,685	3,893
Estimate of DoD's Funding Limits Under the BCA[c]	498	499	511	524	536	549	563	2,568	3,680
Cuts to DoD's Plans Needed to Satisfy the BCA									
CBO projection[a]	0	43	45	46	48	71	79	182	332
FYDP and extension[b]	0	36	33	27	23	45	51	119 [d]	215
2015 Dollars									
CBO Projection[a]	497	533	536	539	541	563	572	2,646	3,781
FYDP and Extension[b]	496	526	525	521	518	539	547	2,586	3,672
Estimate of DoD's Funding Limits Under the BCA[c]	498	491	493	496	497	498	501	2,474	3,473
Cuts to DoD's Plans Needed to Satisfy the BCA									
CBO projection[a]	0	43	43	43	44	64	71	173	308
FYDP and extension[b]	0	35	32	26	21	41	46	114	200

Source: Congressional Budget Office.

Note: DoD = Department of Defense; FYDP = Future Years Defense Program; BCA = Budget Control Act of 2011 as modified by the Bipartisan Budget Act of 2013.

a.   The CBO projection of the base budget incorporates costs that are consistent with DoD's historical experience.

b.   For the extension of the FYDP from 2020 to 2030, CBO projects the costs of DoD's plans using the department's estimates of costs to the extent they are available and costs that are consistent with CBO's projections of price and compensation trends in the overall economy when the department's estimates are not available.

c.   The estimate assumes that DoD would receive 95.5 percent of the BCA's funding limit for national defense, which corresponds to DoD's average share of that funding in base budgets since 2001.

d.   According to DoD's estimates, costs would exceed BCA limits by $115 billion from 2016 through 2019. That total is lower than CBO's estimate for the FYDP and extension because DoD assumes that it will receive a slightly larger share of national defense funding.

the nuclear aircraft carrier *George Washington* (CVN-73)—which was included in last year's FYDP— was not included in the 2015 FYDP.[5] Similarly, the Air Force would retire its fleets of A-10 and U-2 aircraft and defer replacement of its combat search and rescue helicopters.[6]

5.   The Navy's 2015 budget documents indicate that the decision about whether to refuel and overhaul the *George Washington* has been deferred until the 2016 budget.

6.   In April 2014, DoD issued a report, *Estimated Impacts of Sequestration-Level Funding* (http://go.usa.gov/vXWR; PDF, 654 KB), describing additional changes it might make to its plans if its budgets for 2016 through 2019 were constrained by the BCA's limits for those years.

It is not clear whether those reductions in force structure included in the FYDP will ultimately be carried out. Since the 2015 FYDP was released, the Army has indicated its intention to keep its active end strength (the number of military personnel on the rolls as of the final day of a fiscal year) at about 440,000 to 450,000 soldiers (20,000 to 30,000 more than shown in the FYDP), the Navy has stated that it now intends to refuel the *George Washington*, and the Air Force is proceeding with its program to purchase new combat search and rescue helicopters. Unless other parts of DoD's budget are reduced, the reversal of those and any of the other proposed cuts would increase the mismatch between the costs of DoD's plans and the BCA's limits on funding. For example, the Navy estimates that not retiring the *George Washington*

Figure 1-3.

Costs of DoD's Plans as a Share of Economic Output

Percentage of Gross Domestic Product

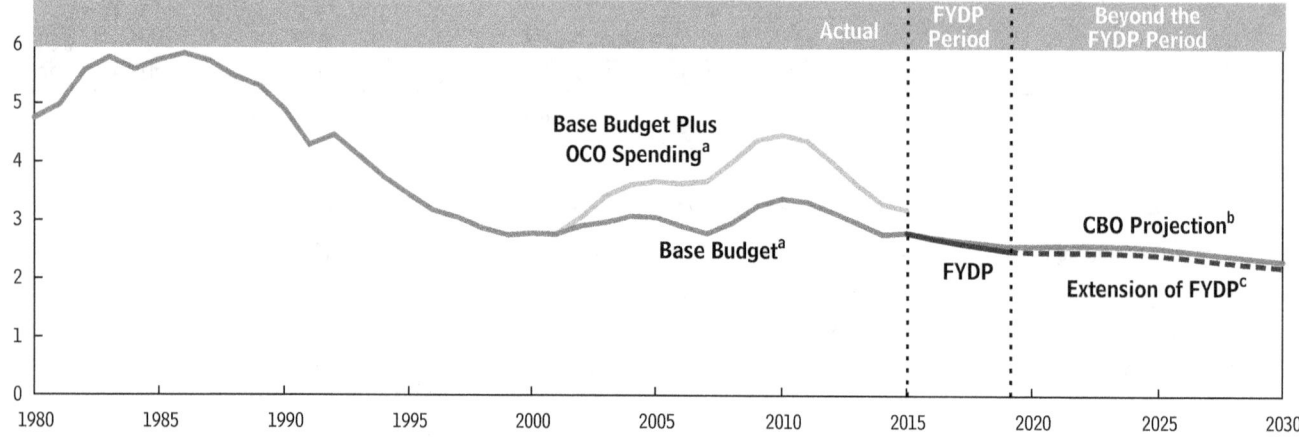

Source: Congressional Budget Office.

Notes: For this figure, estimates describe outlays (as opposed to total obligational authority, which is depicted in the other figures).

DoD = Department of Defense; FYDP = Future Years Defense Program; OCO = overseas contingency operations; FYDP period = 2015 through 2019, the period for which DoD's plans are fully specified.

a. Base-budget data include supplemental and emergency funding before 2002. For 2002 to 2015, supplemental and emergency spending for overseas contingency operations, such as those in Afghanistan and Iraq, and for other purposes is shown separately from the base-budget data. No OCO funding is shown for 2016 and later.

b. The CBO projection of the base budget incorporates costs that are consistent with DoD's historical experience.

c. For the extension of the FYDP from 2020 to 2030, CBO projects the costs of DoD's plans using the department's estimates of costs to the extent they are available and costs that are consistent with CBO's projections of price and compensation trends in the overall economy when the department's estimates are not available.

(and not eliminating a corresponding air wing) would add about $7 billion in costs through 2019 relative to the FYDP. CBO estimates that maintaining Army end strength at 450,000 soldiers would add, relative to the FYDP, $6 billion in costs for military personnel (and additional costs for O&M to support those soldiers) through 2019.

After 2015, if the Congress appropriates an amount for DoD's base budget that is consistent with the BCA's limits on funding for national defense, there would be no sequestration (the cancellation of budgetary resources after they have been appropriated) of base-budget funding or funding for overseas contingency operations. However, if the Congress appropriates more than the BCA allows for the base budget, the difference between the appropriated amounts and the BCA's limit in each year would be subject to sequestration. In that case, funding for overseas contingency operations might also be subject to sequestration.

Costs of DoD's Plans in a Broader Context

CBO's analysis is intended to highlight the long-term budgetary implications of DoD's plans as specified in the 2015 FYDP; it is not an evaluation of the affordability of those plans or of the relationship between those plans and the nation's defense needs. When assessing the affordability of defense plans, some analysts consider the federal government's overall budget situation, including the costs of other federal programs and the amount of revenues being collected, while other analysts focus on the share of overall economic output (as measured by gross domestic product, or GDP) that is being used for defense.

Although the cost of DoD's base-budget plans would increase under the CBO projection, that increase would not be as rapid as the growth of the economy that CBO projects, so spending would decline over time as a share of GDP (see Figure 1-3).[7] Spending for DoD as a share of

---

7. In this section, estimates describe outlays rather than total obligational authority.

GDP fell from an average of 5.5 percent in the 1980s to an average of 3.7 percent in the 1990s. Including supplemental and emergency spending for the wars in Iraq and Afghanistan, DoD's spending as a share of GDP rose above 4 percent after 2007, peaking at 4.5 percent in 2010.

According to the CBO projection of the base budget, the cost of DoD's plans would decline from 2.8 percent of GDP in 2015 to 2.6 percent by 2019 and 2.3 percent by 2030. Any future spending for overseas contingency operations would increase the share of GDP spent on defense above those amounts, holding all else equal.

Costs for Overseas Contingency Operations

Operations in Afghanistan and elsewhere overseas are continuing, and those operations, along with new operations in Iraq and Syria and any others that might arise, will increase total costs relative to DoD's base budget. From 2001 to 2014, DoD's appropriations for overseas contingency operations totaled about $1.7 trillion (in 2015 dollars), an average of about $120 billion per year, or about 20 percent of the department's total funding during that period.

DoD has requested $59 billion for OCO in 2015. Of that total, $29 billion would pay for operations and support of U.S. forces in Afghanistan. The remainder would be allocated to related activities such as repairing or replacing worn equipment, supporting coalition military forces, and conducting other counterterrorism operations.

Some overseas operations are expected to continue after 2015, but the FYDP does not include estimates of the funding that might be requested to support them in those years. DoD has specified in some of its other budget documents a notional value of $30 billion a year to illustrate the potential implications of OCO funding for its overall budget from 2016 through 2019, but those estimates were released before the start of recent operations in Iraq and Syria. Actual amounts requested and appropriated for those years will depend on how overseas operations evolve over time. Funding designated for overseas contingency operations is not constrained by the caps established in the BCA.

Projections of Operation and Support Costs

Appropriations for operation and support fund the compensation for most of the Department of Defense's civilian employees, the majority of costs of the military's health care program, and most of the day-to-day operations of the military. Such funding is the sum of the appropriations for military personnel and for operation and maintenance (O&M).[1] For 2015, DoD requested $336 billion in its base budget for operation and support (O&S), about two-thirds of the total base-budget request.

The Congressional Budget Office projection for the cost of DoD's plans for O&S for 2015 is also $336 billion. According to the CBO projection, operation and support costs would rise to $345 billion (in 2015 dollars) in 2016 and remain at about that level in real (inflation-adjusted) terms through 2019 because growth in costs per person for military pay, military medical care, and other support would be offset by declines in the number of military personnel (see Figure 2-1). In contrast, in the 2015 Future Years Defense Program, DoD estimates that real costs for O&S would rise to $342 billion in 2016 and then fall slightly to an average of $338 billion from 2017 through 2019. The difference in estimates stems primarily from CBO's projections of faster growth in the cost of providing medical care to military personnel and their families and higher pay raises for military personnel.

Assuming that the numbers of major combat units (Army divisions, Navy ships, Air Force squadrons, and so forth) and personnel remain the same as in DoD's plans for 2019, CBO projects that, after 2019, real costs for O&S would rise steadily to $398 billion by 2030. Average annual growth in such costs between 2019 and 2030 would be 1.4 percent. As a result, O&S costs would be 18 percent higher in 2030 than in 2015, and such costs would continue to represent more than 60 percent of the total cost of DoD's plans. Costs would be a little lower—$389 billion in 2030—under the FYDP and extension. Most of the difference in costs between the CBO projection and the FYDP and extension would occur by 2019; after that year, the difference grows only a little because CBO used the same assumptions in both projections for pay raises and for the rate of growth in the cost of medical care (see Table 1-1 on page 8).

DoD has requested an additional $53 billion in O&S funding for 2015 to continue supporting the overseas contingency operations in Afghanistan and elsewhere. Additionally, the Administration's proposed Opportunity, Growth, and Security Initiative includes $11 billion in funding for O&S. CBO did not analyze either of those funding requests because they are not part of DoD's base-budget request.

Projection Methods

CBO estimated the future O&S costs of DoD's plans in three parts:

■ Cash compensation (pay, cash benefits, and retirement benefits) for military personnel and DoD's civilian employees,

■ Medical care for active-duty and retired military personnel and their families, and

■ All other categories of O&M costs, such as fuel, repairs, and spare parts.

---

1. For this analysis, the Congressional Budget Office folded the amounts appropriated for most revolving funds, such as the one for the Defense Commissary Agency, into the appropriation for operation and maintenance. The exception is amounts in the National Defense Sealift Fund that were used to purchase ships prior to 2015, which CBO treated as acquisition. Appropriations in the base budget for revolving funds have averaged less than $3 billion per year since 1980.

Figure 2-1.

Costs of DoD's Operation and Support Plans

Billions of 2015 Dollars

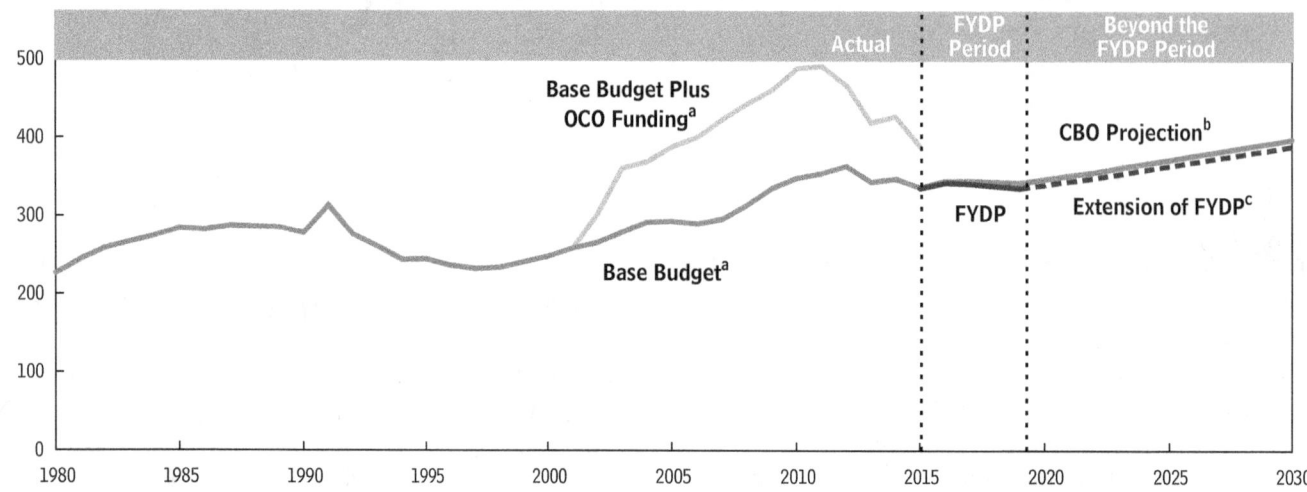

Source: Congressional Budget Office.

Note: DoD = Department of Defense; FYDP = Future Years Defense Program; OCO = overseas contingency operations; FYDP period =
2015 through 2019, the period for which DoD's plans are fully specified.

a.   Base-budget data include supplemental and emergency funding before 2002. For 2002 to 2015, supplemental and emergency funding
for overseas contingency operations, such as those in Afghanistan and Iraq, and for other purposes is shown separately from the
base-budget data. No OCO funding is shown for 2016 and later.

b.   The CBO projection of the base budget incorporates costs that are consistent with DoD's historical experience.

c.   For the extension of the FYDP from 2020 to 2030, CBO projects the costs of DoD's plans using the department's estimates of costs to the
extent they are available and costs that are consistent with CBO's projections of price and compensation trends in the overall economy
when the department's estimates are not available.

Cash compensation constitutes the largest of the three components in the 2015 budget request, accounting for more than half of the requested appropriation for O&S. Funding for compensation comes from the appropriations for military personnel and for O&M.

Medical care for military personnel, military retirees, and their families is also funded largely from the military personnel and O&M appropriation accounts. Under the CBO projection, the cost of such care grows more quickly than cash compensation through 2030.

The third component includes the purchase of items ranging from office supplies to aircraft fuel but excludes ships, tanks, aircraft, and other major pieces of equipment, which are purchased through the procurement accounts. It also includes the purchase of services, such as contracts with private entities to maintain facilities, prepare food, repair weapon systems, operate information systems, and conduct many other activities.

CBO estimated costs for cash compensation and medical care in a "bottom-up" manner by combining estimates of the numbers of people who will receive cash compensation and be eligible for medical care, enrollment and participation rates in different health care plans, and various factors relating to cost and price. Such estimates were not possible for the third component of O&S costs because of the wide array of items and services purchased. Consequently, for those costs, CBO used DoD's estimates through 2019 and projected costs from 2019 to 2030 on the basis of DoD's historical experience. (See Box 2-1 for a discussion of how O&M costs have grown over the years.)

The Numbers of Military and Civilian Personnel

The size of the military is a significant factor in DoD's costs for O&S. Changing the number of military personnel directly affects the costs to compensate, train, equip,

Table 2-1.

DoD's Plans for the Number of Military and Civilian Personnel, 2014 to 2019

Thousands of Personnel

	2014	FYDP Period					Change in Personnel from 2014 to 2019	
		2015	2016	2017	2018	2019	Thousands	Percent
Military Personnel								
Army								
Active force	510 ᵃ	490 ᵃ	470	450	430	420	-90	-18
Reserve and National Guard	556	552	531	519	507	500	-56	-10
Navy								
Active force	324	324	321	323	323	323	*	**
Reserve	57	55	55	56	57	57	*	**
Marine Corps								
Active force	190 ᵃ	184 ᵃ	179	175	175	175	-15	-8
Reserve	42	41	41	40	40	40	-1	-3
Air Force								
Active force	328	311	310	309	309	309	-19	-6
Reserve and National Guard	176	172	173	170	170	170	-6	-3
All Services								
Active force	1,352	1,309	1,281	1,257	1,237	1,227	-125	-9
Reserve and National Guard	831	821	800	786	774	767	-63	-8
Total	**2,183**	**2,129**	**2,081**	**2,042**	**2,011**	**1,994**	**-188**	**-9**
Civilian Personnel	778	771	764	758	748	741	-37	-5

Source: Congressional Budget Office.

Notes: The Department of Defense (DoD) measures the size of its force in terms of end strength—the number of military personnel on the rolls as of the final day of a fiscal year.

FYDP = Future Years Defense Program; * = between -500 and zero personnel; ** = between -0.5 percent and zero.

a.   In 2015, the Army and the Marine Corps intend to continue their practice from previous years and fund a small number of active-duty military personnel through the budgets for overseas contingency operations. This table includes those personnel, but the costs of those personnel are not included in the base budget.

and support those personnel. DoD measures the size of its force in terms of end strength—the number of military personnel as of the final day of the fiscal year. Relative to 2014 personnel levels, DoD's 2015 plan would shrink the total size of its force by 9 percent by 2019 (see Table 2-1). Between 2014 and 2019, the plan indicates a decrease in end strength of about 125,000 personnel in the active force and about 63,000 personnel in the reserve and National Guard.

Although each of the services would cut end strength under DoD's 2015 plan, roughly three-quarters of the total reduction would occur in the Army. From 2014 to 2019, the Army's active-duty end strength would drop from 510,400 to 420,000, and its end strength in the reserve and National Guard would fall from 556,200 to 500,000. Over the same period, the Air Force's active-duty end strength would be reduced from 327,600 to 308,800, and its end strength in the reserve and the Air National Guard would fall from 175,800 to 170,100. (Most of the reduction in Air Force personnel would occur by the end of 2015.) The number of active-duty Marine Corps personnel would decrease from 190,200 to 175,000. The sizes of the active-duty Navy, Navy Reserve, and Marine Corps Reserve would decline only slightly.

Box 2-1.

Comparing Historical and Projected Growth of Spending for Operation and Maintenance per Service Member

Appropriations for operation and maintenance (O&M) fund the day-to-day operations of the military, including equipment maintenance, training, civilian compensation, and most of the costs for military medical care. O&M costs per active-duty service member have increased rapidly in the past and are projected to continue to do so in both the Congressional Budget Office (CBO) projection and the extension of the Future Years Defense Program (FYDP).

From 1980 to 2001 (the last year before the onset of major combat operations in Afghanistan and Iraq), O&M costs per active-duty service member nearly doubled, from $57,000 to $110,000, after adjusting to remove the effects of inflation (see the figure). Notably, the cost per active-duty service member grew by a roughly constant amount of $2,300 a year despite broad shifts in defense funding, such as the military buildup of the 1980s and the reduction in forces at the end of the Cold War.

The overseas operations that began after 2001, funded largely through supplemental and emergency appropriations and not through the base budget, caused rapid growth in O&M costs. O&M funding per active-duty service member quickly departed from the historical trend as a result of the cost of conducting major operations, the wear and tear on

equipment in combat, and the large number of reserve and National Guard personnel deployed. (Because CBO's calculation involved dividing all O&M costs by the number of active-duty service members, supporting more deployed reserve and National Guard personnel increased the O&M cost per active-duty service member.) By 2010, O&M costs per active-duty service member had doubled again, reaching $225,000, including costs for overseas contingency operations.

The large growth in O&M funding to support operations in Afghanistan and Iraq obscures another significant development since 2001—the base budget's departure from the historical trend of O&M costs per active-duty service member. By 2014, O&M costs per active-duty service member in the base budget were $148,000, about $13,000 above what is implied by the trend between 1980 and 2001.

During the FYDP period, O&M costs per active-duty service member are projected to rise by an average of more than $4,000 per year, from $153,000 in 2015 to $170,000 in 2019, or an average of $23,000 above what is implied by the historical trend. That rapid rise coincides with a planned 6 percent decline in active-duty end strength (the number of military personnel on the rolls as of the final day of a fiscal year).

Continued

DoD also plans to reduce the size of its civilian workforce. DoD's plan would reduce the number of "direct hire" civilians from 778,000 in 2014 to 741,000 in 2019, a decline of 5 percent. Direct hire civilians are employees hired directly by DoD, and they include foreign nationals hired to support DoD activities in their home countries.

Pay, Cash Benefits, and Accrual Payments for Retirement Benefits

Pay and cash benefits for military service members include basic pay, reenlistment bonuses, food and housing allowances, and various other elements. Basic pay,

which is determined by the service member's pay grade and years of service, is the single largest and most visible component of cash pay. DoD's appropriation for military personnel is also charged for accrual payments to the Military Retirement Fund; those payments are calculated to provide a balance in the fund that would pay for future retirement benefits to current military personnel. (Health care benefits available to service members and their families through the Military Health System are considered in the next section of this chapter.) DoD employs roughly 800,000 full-time-equivalent civilian workers, most of whom are paid from the O&M account.

Box 2-1.   **Continued**

Comparing Historical and Projected Growth of Spending for
Operation and Maintenance per Service Member

Costs of Operation and Maintenance per Active-Duty Service Member

Thousands of 2015 Dollars

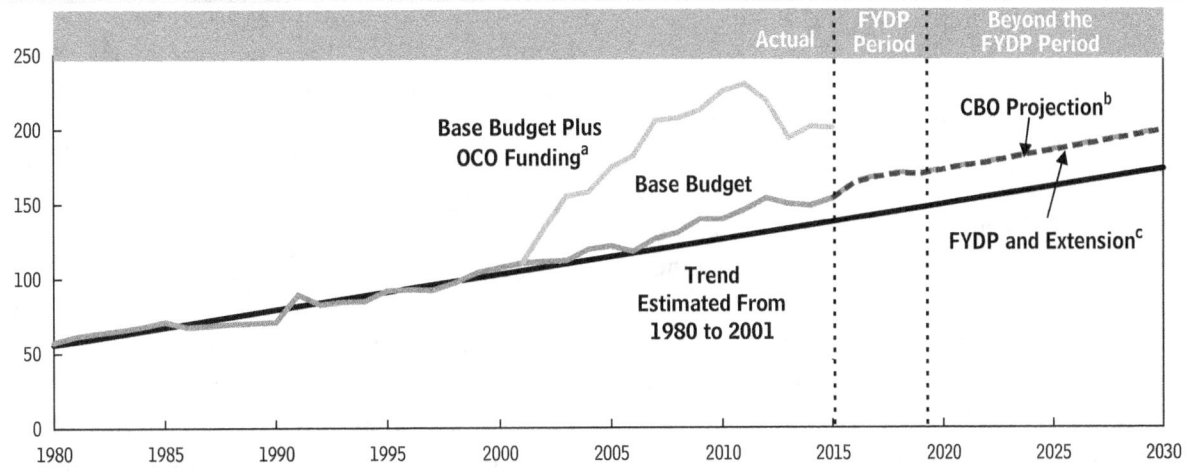

Source: Congressional Budget Office.

Note: FYDP = Future Years Defense Program; FYDP period = 2015 to 2019, the years for which the Department of Defense's
(DoD's) plans are fully specified.

a.   For 2002 to 2015, supplemental and emergency funding for overseas contingency operations (OCO), such as those in
Afghanistan and Iraq, and for other purposes is shown separately from the base-budget data. No OCO funding is shown for 2016
and later.

b.   The CBO projection of the base budget incorporates costs that are consistent with DoD's historical experience.

c.   For the extension of the FYDP from 2020 to 2030, CBO projects the costs of DoD's plans using the department's estimates of
costs to the extent they are available and costs that are consistent with CBO's projections of price and compensation trends in
the overall economy when the department's estimates are not available.

Beyond the FYDP period, projected growth in O&M costs per active-duty service member slows substantially from the rate projected in the FYDP, although it still exceeds the historical rate of $2,300 per year. From 2019 to 2030, such costs grow by more than $2,600, annually, in both the CBO projection and the FYDP and extension. Those projections assume that active-duty end strength does not change after 2019. Therefore, the growth in O&M costs per service member stems entirely from CBO's projection of growth in the total O&M budget (specifically, growth of civilian compensation, portions of the Military Health System, and other O&M). Throughout those years, O&M costs per service member would average about $25,000 above the amount implied by the historical trend, or about $2,000 more than the average during the FYDP period.

The Administration's 2015 budget request includes $203 billion in O&S funding for pay and benefits for DoD's military personnel and most of its civilian employees. About $135 billion of that total is in the appropriation for military personnel, which supports DoD's active-duty service members plus planned training activities for reserve and National Guard members (but not their potential activations for overseas conflicts, which are funded outside of the base budget). CBO estimates that an additional $68 billion to compensate most of DoD's civilian workers will come from the appropriation for O&M.[2] DoD projects that annual costs to compensate military and civilian personnel will decline to about $191 billion (in 2015 dollars) in 2019, reflecting a combination of the planned reductions in personnel levels and planned growth in pay below the projected rate of inflation. Under the FYDP and extension, CBO estimates that those costs would grow by an average of 1.3 percent per year in real terms after 2019, and reach $219 billion in 2030.

According to the CBO projection of DoD's plans, the real costs of compensation in O&S would decline slightly over the FYDP period, starting at $204 billion in 2015 and ending at $197 billion in 2019 (see Table 2-2). Those estimates are higher than the costs shown in the FYDP because they incorporate the assumption that military pay raises would be higher than what DoD proposes for most of those years, although civilian pay raises would match those planned in the FYDP. After 2019, CBO estimates, compensation costs would grow by an average of 1.3 percent per year in real terms, reaching $227 billion by 2030.

Since 2004, growth in the employment cost index (ECI) for private-sector wages and salaries has provided a benchmark for the adjustment to the military basic pay table that takes place at the start of each calendar year. For calendar years 2004 through 2006, the pay raise was stipulated as equal to the recent percentage increase in the ECI plus 0.5 percentage points. From calendar year 2007 forward, the law has set the pay raise equal to the recent percentage increase in the ECI, without the additional 0.5 percentage points, unless that raise is overridden by the Congress.[3] As it turned out, the 10 annual pay raises that took effect between calendar years 2001 and 2010 all exceeded the corresponding percentage change in the

ECI by at least 0.5 percentage points. For example, for calendar years 2007 through 2010, DoD requested a pay raise equal to the percentage increase in the ECI—the value that would have prevailed by default without Congressional action—but the Congress overrode (and the President acceded to) a pay raise equal to the percentage increase in the ECI plus 0.5 percentage points. More recently, for calendar years 2011 through 2013, DoD continued to request pay raises equal to the recent percentage increases in the ECI, and those raises were enacted. For calendar year 2014, DoD requested a pay raise of 1.0 percent (less than the 1.8 percent increase in the ECI), and that smaller raise took effect.

For military pay raises during the FYDP period, DoD's plan includes increases that would fall short of the department's projections of the growth rate of the ECI.[4] For calendar year 2015, DoD is again requesting a pay raise of 1.0 percent for military personnel. DoD's plan includes raises of 1.0 percent for calendar years 2016 and 2017, 1.5 percent for calendar year 2018, and 1.8 percent for calendar year 2019. In the FYDP and extension, CBO assumed that military pay raises would follow the pattern indicated in the FYDP through 2019 and then equal the percentage increases in the ECI (the default outcome as stipulated in current law) from 2020 through 2030. In the CBO projection, CBO assumed that the military pay raise would be 1.0 percent in 2015, consistent with both DoD's plan and Congressional action to date.[5] For the remainder of the FYDP period (2016 through 2019) and the duration of the projection (through 2030), the CBO projection follows the long-standing historical pattern under which military pay raises keep pace with the growth in the ECI.

---

2. Compensation for some civilian employees—about $8 billion in 2015—is paid from other appropriations and not included in the totals for O&M. For instance, some civilians in military laboratories are paid from the appropriation for research, development, test, and evaluation.

3. 37 U.S.C. 1009 (adjustments of monthly basic pay) states that the percentage increase in basic pay for a given calendar year is equal to the percentage increase in the ECI for private-sector wages and salaries from the third calendar quarter three years prior to the effective date of the pay raise to the third calendar quarter two years prior to the effective date.

4. Department of Defense, *Fiscal Year 2015 Budget Request: Overview* (March 2014), p. 5-5, http://go.usa.gov/vP59 (PDF, 2.43 MB).

5. The House of Representatives passed its version of the National Defense Authorization Act for 2015 (H.R. 4435) in May 2014. That act acceded to DoD's request, although dissatisfaction with that request was expressed; see U.S. House of Representatives, Armed Services Committee, *Fact Sheet: Highlights of the Chairman's Mark, H.R. 4435 National Defense Authorization Act for Fiscal Year 2015* (May 5, 2014), p. 4, http://go.usa.gov/ACez (PDF, 372 KB). The Senate has not yet taken up its version of the act, but the bill that passed the Senate Committee on Armed Services (S. 2410) in May 2014 also acceded to DoD's request.

For civilian pay raises, DoD's plan includes increases equal to those requested for military personnel for all years included in the FYDP.[6] CBO adopted DoD's plan for civilian pay raises through 2019 for both the CBO projection and the FYDP and extension. Because the CBO projection for 2016 through 2019 pegs the military (but not civilian) pay raises to the ECI, the military pay raises exceed the civilian pay raises for that projection over those four years. CBO assumed in both projections that, starting in 2019, the civilian pay raise would be pegged to increases in the ECI and thereby track the military pay raise.

The Military Health System

More than 9 million people are eligible for health care through DoD's TRICARE program. Eligible beneficiaries as of 2014 included 1.6 million military personnel from active components or activated members of the reserve or National Guard, 2.2 million family members of those personnel, and 5.3 million military retirees and their family members. Beneficiaries may seek free or subsidized care from military treatment facilities, regional networks of civilian providers under contract with TRICARE, or other civilian providers. DoD also manages TRICARE for Life, a program that the Congress authorized in the 2001 National Defense Authorization Act (NDAA) to supplement Medicare for beneficiaries eligible for both Medicare and the military health benefit.[7]

This report does not consider the costs of the health care or other benefits provided to veterans by the Department of Veterans Affairs (VA). That department's budget request for 2015 is $164 billion, including $65 billion to provide health care to veterans who have service-connected disabilities or who meet certain other

criteria for eligibility.[8] Other VA benefits include monthly cash payments that compensate for service-connected disabilities and GI Bill benefits that reimburse some of the costs of higher education.[9] While TRICARE benefits are available to all of the roughly 2 million retired service members—most of whom served for 20 years or more—and their eligible family members, VA benefits are potentially available to the much larger population of 22 million veterans who received honorable or general discharges from their (typically shorter) military service.

DoD requested $46 billion in O&S funding for military health care in 2015, about 9 percent of the total funding requested for the department's base budget.[10] Under the CBO projection, the costs of DoD's plans for the military health system for 2015 would be slightly higher, about $47 billion, because that projection incorporates the assumption that the Congress will not adopt DoD's proposals for reducing the department's costs; the Congress has rejected related proposals and frozen various enrollment fees, deductibles, and copayments each year since 2007.[11] CBO projects that the costs of the Military

---

6. CBO compared the annual pay raises of the two groups between 1984 and 2014. For the military pay raises, CBO included across-the-board pay raises as well as the average increases in years in which pay raises contained additional amounts for particular grades or seniority levels. For the civilian pay raises, CBO included across-the-board pay raises as well as the average increases in locality pay. Over those 31 years, the military pay raises were larger in 12 instances, the civil service pay raises were larger in 2 instances, and the raises were equal in the remaining 17 instances.

7. For more on the military health system, see Congressional Budget Office, *Approaches to Reducing Federal Spending on Military Health Care* (January 2014), www.cbo.gov/publication/44993.

8. The Veterans Access, Choice, and Accountability Act of 2014 (Public Law 113-146), enacted in August 2014, contains provisions that, among other things, authorize additional medical care for veterans outside of VA's own facilities if those veterans are unable to schedule appointments at VA facilities within the department's wait-time goals or if the veterans reside beyond a specified distance from the nearest VA facility. For CBO's estimates of the budgetary effects of that act, see Congressional Budget Office, letter to the Honorable Bernie Sanders providing an estimate for H.R. 3230, Veterans Access, Choice, and Accountability Act of 2014 (July 29, 2014), www.cbo.gov/publication/45601.

9. For more on VA's disability compensation program, see Congressional Budget Office, *Veterans' Disability Compensation: Trends and Policy Options* (August 2014), www.cbo.gov/publication/45615.

10. Neither DoD's request of $46 billion in O&S funding nor CBO's projection of O&S costs includes relatively small amounts that the military health system is provided for procurement, military construction, and research, development, test, and evaluation (a total of $1.5 billion in DoD's request for 2015). The CBO projection includes those costs in the totals for the latter three appropriation accounts.

11. For the legislative history of cost-sharing proposals for TRICARE, see Congressional Budget Office, *Costs of Military Pay and Benefits in the Defense Budget* (November 2012), Appendix C, www.cbo.gov/publication/43574.

Table 2-2.

CBO Projection of Operation and Support Costs in DoD's Base Budget, 2015 and 2019

Billions of 2015 Dollars

	2015	2019
Military Personnel		
Military personnel in the MHS	9	9
TRICARE for Life accrual payments	7	8
Other military personnel	120	117
Total	**136**	**133**
Operation and Maintenance		
Civilian personnel		
Civilian personnel in the MHS	5	5
Other civilian personnel	63	59
Subtotal	68	64
O&M in the MHS excluding civilian personnel	27	29
Other O&M[a]	106	117
Total	**200**	**209**
Total Appropriations for Operation and Support	**336**	**342**
Memorandum:		
Military Health System		
Military personnel in the MHS	9	9
TRICARE for Life accrual payments	7	8
Civilian personnel in the MHS	5	5
O&M in the MHS excluding civilian personnel	27	29
Total[b]	**47**	**50**
Compensation[c]		
Military personnel	136	133
Civilian personnel	68	64
Total[d]	**204**	**197**

Source: Congressional Budget Office.

Notes: The CBO projection applies CBO's estimates of costs that are consistent with DoD's historical experience.

   DoD = Department of Defense; MHS = Military Health System; O&M = operation and maintenance.

a.   For this analysis, CBO folded appropriations for most revolving funds (such as the one for the Defense Commissary Agency) into the appropriations for operation and maintenance.

b.   These figures do not include MHS spending in accounts other than operation and support.

c.   Compensation consists of pay, cash benefits, and accrual payments for retirement benefits. For civilians, it also includes DoD's contributions for health insurance.

d.   These figures do not include compensation for civilian personnel funded from accounts other than operation and support.

Health System (in 2015 dollars) would reach $50 billion by 2019 and $65 billion by 2030 (see Figure 2-2). Although the FYDP indicates that spending for the Military Health System will grow at an average annual rate of 0.8 percent above the rate of inflation from 2015 to 2019, the CBO projection implies average annual growth of 1.3 percent over the same period. Over the entire projection period from 2015 to 2030, the CBO projection shows an average real growth rate of spending for the Military Health System of 2.2 percent per year.

Major Budget Categories

DoD's budget documents delineate medical costs in five major categories:

Figure 2-2.

Costs of DoD's Plans for Its Military Health System

Billions of 2015 Dollars

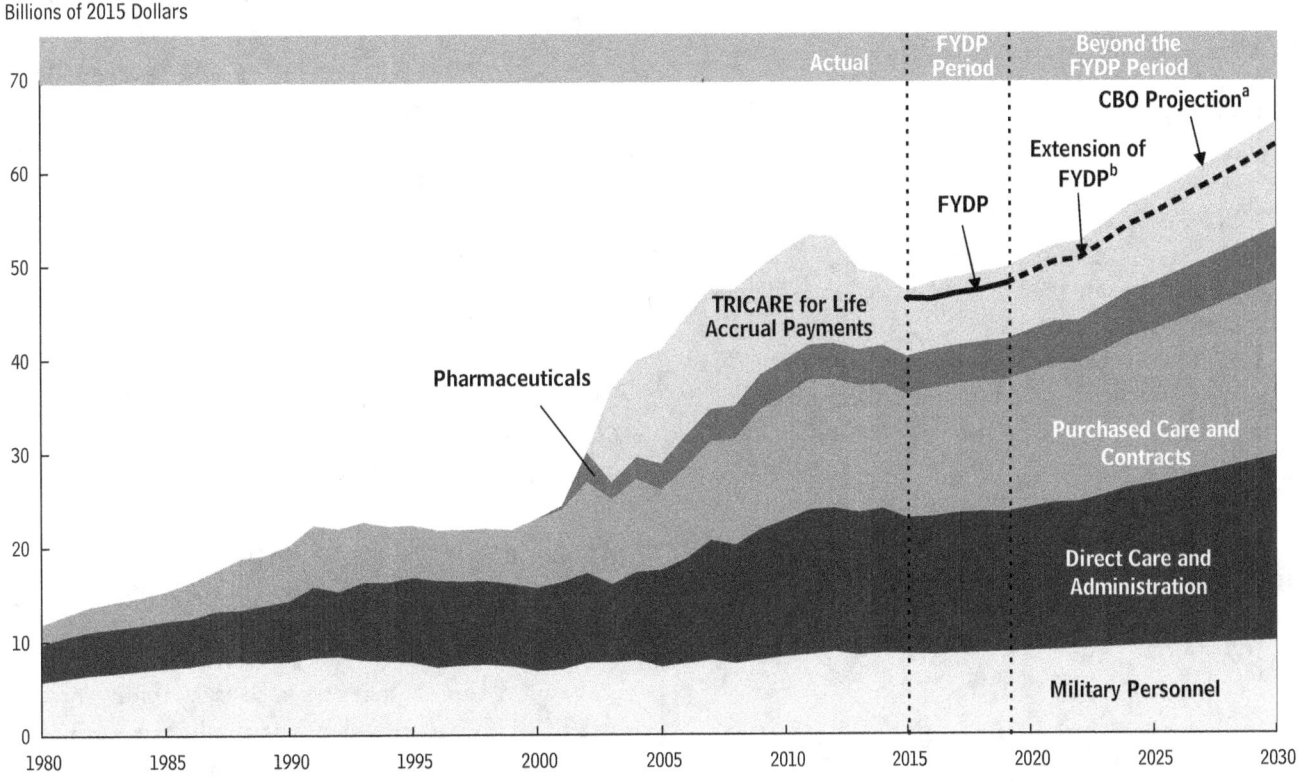

Source: Congressional Budget Office.

Notes: Supplemental and emergency funding for overseas contingency operations, such as those in Afghanistan and Iraq, is included for 2014 and earlier but not for later years.

Before 2001, pharmaceutical costs were not separately identifiable but were embedded in the costs of two categories: "Purchased Care and Contracts" and "Direct Care and Administration." In 2001 and later years, most pharmaceutical costs are separately identifiable, but some of those costs are embedded in the category "TRICARE for Life Accrual Payments."

The amounts shown for the Future Years Defense Program (FYDP) and the extension of the FYDP are the totals for all categories.

DoD = Department of Defense; FYDP period = 2015 through 2019, the period for which DoD's plans are fully specified.

a. Each category shows the CBO projection of the base budget from 2015 to 2030. That projection incorporates costs that are consistent with DoD's historical experience.

b. For the extension of the FYDP from 2020 to 2030, CBO projects the costs of DoD's plans using the department's estimates of costs to the extent they are available and costs that are consistent with CBO's projections of price and compensation trends in the overall economy when the department's estimates are not available.

■ *Military personnel* covers the costs of pay and benefits for uniformed personnel assigned to work in the Military Health System. Those costs are included in CBO's tally of the total cost of the system, but they are counted only once in CBO's projection of overall O&S costs (see Table 2-2).[12]

■ *Direct care and administration* covers the operation of military medical facilities and other administrative and training activities. The category includes pay and

benefits for civilian personnel assigned to work in those facilities but excludes pay and benefits for military personnel who work in those facilities because those costs are counted in the previous category.

---

12. For example, the same $9 billion of funding for military personnel in the Military Health System in 2015 appears twice in Table 2-2, once under the military personnel appropriation and again as part of the cost of the Military Health System.

■ *Purchased care and contracts* covers medical care delivered by providers in the private sector, both inside and outside of the TRICARE network.

■ *Pharmaceuticals* covers purchases of medicines dispensed at military medical facilities, at pharmacies inside and outside of DoD's network, and through DoD's mail-order pharmacy program.

■ *TRICARE for Life accrual payments* covers funds deducted from DoD's military personnel appropriation and credited to the Medicare-Eligible Retiree Health Care Fund. Outlays from that fund are used for two purposes—to reimburse military medical facilities for care provided to military retirees and their family members who are also eligible for Medicare, and to cover most of the out-of-pocket costs that those beneficiaries would otherwise incur when seeking care from private-sector Medicare providers. (Those payments are included in the cost of military personnel and in CBO's tally of the total cost of the Military Health System, but they are counted only once in CBO's projection of overall O&S costs.)

The costs of the Military Health System may be organized in various ways depending on the purpose of the analysis. One way is to extract the costs of civilian personnel from the accounts for direct care and administration in order to highlight the respective costs of military and civilian personnel in the system and elsewhere in DoD's base budget (see Table 2-2 on page 24). However, in CBO's assessment, more useful projections can be generated by using a taxonomy of costs that corresponds more closely to the functions performed by the Military Health System than to the budgetary accounts through which the system is funded.

Therefore, CBO projects the costs of the military health system in three categories: military personnel, TRICARE for Life accrual payments, and the combination of direct care and administration, purchased care and contracts, and pharmaceuticals. The latter components are grouped together because they tend to be driven by common factors, such as the number of beneficiaries in the TRICARE program and cost trends in the nation's health care system as a whole.

Policy Proposals

Military retirees and their families generally pay much less for health care than comparable civilian families.[13]

DoD estimated that in 2013, a typical military retiree could enroll his or her family in TRICARE Prime for $540 per year and would, on average, pay an additional $435 in copayments and other fees for a total annual cost of $975. In contrast, DoD estimated that a civilian in the general U.S. population who enrolled in a family plan with a health maintenance organization (HMO) offered by an employer in that year would typically pay $4,940 as the employee's share of the annual premium. With deductibles and copayments averaging $965, that family would pay a total of $5,905 over the course of the year. Thus, the family enrolled in a civilian HMO would pay costs that are six times as high as what a similar family would pay for coverage in TRICARE Prime. On the basis of a parallel calculation, DoD estimated that a family who used a civilian preferred-provider organization (PPO) would pay more than five times what a similar military family would pay for coverage in TRICARE Standard (which operates as a traditional fee-for-service plan) or Extra (which operates as a PPO).[14]

As a result of those differences in costs, a rapidly growing share of military retirees and their families are relying on TRICARE rather than participating in health insurance provided by civilian employers or purchasing insurance on their own. In 2002, about 43 percent of military retirees signed up for private health insurance, but by 2013, that figure had dropped to 21 percent.[15] In addition, low out-of-pocket costs and other factors have led to usage rates for inpatient and outpatient care among enrollees in TRICARE Prime (the TRICARE option most similar to an HMO) that DoD has found to be higher than usage rates for comparable civilians enrolled in HMOs.[16]

To reduce the rate of growth of its health care costs, DoD's 2015 budget includes the following proposed changes to the TRICARE program, implementation of which would begin in 2015 and be completed by 2019:

13. See Congressional Budget Office, *Approaches to Reducing Federal Spending on Military Health Care* (January 2014), pp. 13–15, www.cbo.gov/publication/44993.

14. See Department of Defense, *Evaluation of the TRICARE Program—Access, Cost, and Quality: Fiscal Year 2014 Report to Congress* (February 2014), p. 89, http://go.usa.gov/vEc4.

15. Ibid., pp. 90 and 92.

16. Ibid., pp. 74 and 79.

- Institute an annual fee for military retirees who are newly eligible for Medicare and who enroll in TRICARE for Life (the fee would not be charged to retirees who are already participating in TRICARE for Life);

- Replace TRICARE Prime, Standard, and Extra (the "triple option" for which TRICARE was originally named) with a single consolidated plan for family members of active-duty service members and for retirees and their family members who are not eligible for Medicare, requiring generally higher deductibles and copayments than exist under the current triple option; and

- Raise the copayments for brand-name drugs and for drugs purchased at retail pharmacies by family members of active-duty service members and by retirees and their families, as a further incentive to purchase generic and mail-order drugs; and require that all prescriptions for long-term maintenance medications (for example, to treat high blood pressure or high cholesterol) be filled at military facilities or through the mail-order pharmacy program.[17]

DoD estimates that those changes would generate savings in 2015 of $94 million in the department's O&M account and $750 million in TRICARE for Life accrual payments; as the policy changes are phased in from 2015 to 2019, total savings of $5.5 billion and $4.1 billion would accrue in those two categories. Those savings are incorporated in the estimates of costs in the FYDP.

The Congress has a long history of denying DoD's requests to increase the costs borne by TRICARE beneficiaries. Indeed, the version of the 2015 NDAA that passed the House of Representatives (H.R. 4435) rejected the proposals delineated above. The full Senate has not yet acted on its version of the NDAA, but the bill that passed the Senate Committee on Armed Services (S. 2410) includes only DoD's proposed changes to pharmacy benefits. Therefore, the CBO projection incorporates the assumption that DoD's current set of proposals will not be adopted.

Projected Costs

For pay and benefits of military personnel who work in the Military Health System, the CBO projection is based on the same series of annual increases as for all other military personnel (discussed above). Military compensation is not a major contributor to the overall increase in costs that CBO projects for the Military Health System because it is smaller than most of the other major categories and is projected to grow less rapidly.

For the costs of direct care and administration, purchased care and contracts, and pharmaceuticals, the CBO projection between 2015 and 2019 uses the estimates from DoD's FYDP with one adjustment: CBO increased the estimated costs for purchased care and pharmaceuticals in the FYDP by the amount that DoD expects to save if its proposals for changes to the TRICARE program are authorized by the Congress. Those proposals would boost the share of costs borne by TRICARE beneficiaries, which is similar to other proposals that DoD has made since 2007 and that the Congress has rejected repeatedly in defense authorization acts. After 2019, costs per beneficiary in those three categories are projected to grow at the same rate that CBO projects for health care costs nationwide apart from the Medicare program (because that program differs in important ways from the rest of the health care system).[18] Over the entire 2015–2030 period, the real annual growth in costs per beneficiary averages 2.1 percent for direct care and administration, 2.3 percent for purchased care and contracts, and 2.4 percent for pharmaceuticals.[19]

For TRICARE for Life accrual payments, the CBO projection is derived from the DoD Office of the Actuary's projection. That office's projection implies that accrual payments would grow at an average annual rate per service member of 3.2 percent (after adjusting to remove the effects of inflation) between 2015 and 2030 if the Congress does not adopt the changes in cost sharing proposed by DoD.

---

17. Department of Defense, *Fiscal Year 2015 Budget Request: Overview* (March 2014), pp. 5-7–5-14, http://go.usa.gov/vP59 (PDF, 2.43 MB).

18. See Congressional Budget Office, *The 2014 Long-Term Budget Outlook* (July 2014), p. 34, www.cbo.gov/publication/45471.

19. In nominal terms, those average annual growth rates for the 2015–2030 period are 4.1 percent for direct care and administration, 4.4 percent for purchased care and contracts, and 4.4 percent for pharmaceuticals. The calculation of the growth rate for pharmaceuticals excludes some pharmacy costs that are not paid explicitly from O&M funds but are embedded in the accrual payments for TRICARE for Life.

All together, the costs of the Military Health System in the CBO projection exceed those in the FYDP and extension by $2 billion in 2030 ($65 billion versus $63 billion). From 2015 through 2019, annual growth rates of costs for military personnel, purchased care, and pharmaceuticals are somewhat higher in the CBO projection: CBO assumes that the Congress will authorize slightly higher pay raises for military personnel and that the Congress will not authorize DoD's proposed changes to beneficiaries' shares of the costs of purchased care and pharmaceuticals. After 2019, growth rates for all categories in the two projections are the same.

Other Operation and Maintenance Costs

The remainder of O&S spending is for other O&M—the portions of operation and maintenance other than those involving the Military Health System and compensation for DoD's civilians. CBO also included appropriations for most revolving funds in the other O&M category. Other O&M costs per active-duty service member have grown steadily since 1980.

CBO's estimates of other O&M costs are identical under the CBO projection and the FYDP and extension. Because a diverse array of functions contribute to other O&M costs, it was not practical for CBO to build an estimate beyond the FYDP period from the bottom up—that is, develop estimates for the costs of the various components involved and then sum up those estimates, as CBO did for the projections of the costs of compensation and military health care. Instead, CBO used a top-down

approach to project other O&M costs for the years beyond the FYDP.

Within the FYDP period, other O&M costs are projected to grow in line with DoD's estimates, from $106 billion in 2015 to $118 billion in 2018 before edging down to $117 billion in 2019. Beyond the FYDP period, CBO projected other O&M costs using the same growth rate as the historical trend in other O&M costs per active-duty service member (from 1980 to 2001, about $1,100 per person per year in 2015 dollars). As a result, other O&M costs would grow steadily to $132 billion in 2030.

The sources of historical growth in other O&M costs cannot be readily determined from the aggregate data and could have been caused by a number of factors. For example, DoD may have increased its hiring of contractors over time—using O&M funds—to provide services and functions that did not exist in earlier years or that had previously been provided by military personnel. Additionally, the costs to operate and maintain weapon systems may have increased. Since the 1990s, the rate of replacement of weapon systems has been slower than it was previously, and that has resulted in increased average ages for many types of weapons in use today. That factor may contribute to the increase observed in O&M costs because older weapon systems can be more costly to maintain as they age, particularly as they approach the end of their service life. In addition, when an older weapon system is replaced by a more modern weapon system, the more modern system may be more expensive to operate early in its service life than was its predecessor because the more modern system has greater capability and technical complexity. That may result in higher O&M costs across generations of weapon systems.

Projections of Acquisition Costs

Acquisition funding is used to develop and purchase weapon systems and other major pieces of equipment and to upgrade the capabilities or extend the service life of weapon systems. Such funding is the sum of the appropriations for procurement and for research, development, test, and evaluation. For 2015, the Administration requested $154 billion for acquisition in the Department of Defense's base budget—31 percent of its total request for DoD's base budget.

Under the Congressional Budget Office projection, the costs to implement DoD's plans for acquisition would rise to $177 billion (in 2015 dollars) in 2016, 15 percent above the amount in 2015 (see Figure 3-1). Those costs would rise to $187 billion in 2019, the final year covered by the Future Years Defense Program. In the years beyond the FYDP period, the costs of DoD's acquisition plans would continue to increase, reaching $220 billion in the early 2020s. Costs would remain near or above $200 billion per year through 2028 but dip to about $190 billion by 2030.

The steep increases in acquisition costs in 2016 and in the years immediately beyond the FYDP period illustrate that DoD has created two classic "bow waves" by constraining acquisition during periods of tight budgets but continuing to plan for more acquisition thereafter. Bow waves beyond the FYDP period had been a common feature of DoD's plans for many years, particularly during periods of flat or declining budgets. For most of the last decade, bow waves largely disappeared because budgets grew steadily. With the Budget Control Act of 2011 restraining the growth of appropriations, however, especially in the near term, a substantial bow wave is again apparent in the years immediately beyond the FYDP period. In addition, the Administration's decision to present plans that adhere to the BCA in 2015 but not in subsequent years has created another bow wave between 2015 and 2016.

Under DoD's estimates for the FYDP, real (inflation-adjusted) acquisition costs would increase 13 percent, to $174 billion, in 2016 but then remain essentially constant between 2016 and 2019. In its extension of the FYDP, CBO estimates that real acquisition costs would increase by an additional 16 percent from 2019 to 2022 but then gradually decline to $174 billion in 2030. From 2020 to 2030, total real costs would be 8 percent lower under the extension of the FYDP than under the CBO projection, primarily because of differences in estimates of the costs of new weapon systems. Specifically, costs for weapon systems that are not yet in full production are typically higher under the CBO projection than under the FYDP and extension because DoD's historical experience shows that the costs of weapon systems are typically higher than estimates made during development.[1]

DoD has requested additional acquisition funding for 2015 to continue supporting the overseas contingency operations in Afghanistan and elsewhere. From 2001 through 2014, about $350 billion (in 2015 dollars) in OCO funding was appropriated for acquisition. Those funds have been used for a variety of purposes, including replacing equipment destroyed in battle and purchasing new types of equipment, such as mine-resistant vehicles. For 2015, $6.1 billion of the $59 billion requested for overseas contingency operations is for acquisition. Of that amount, $6.0 billion is for procurement and about $80 million is for RDT&E. DoD has also requested an

---

1. Historical analysis of DoD's acquisition programs indicates that costs have grown substantially relative to initial estimates. See Mark V. Arena and others, *Historical Cost Growth of Completed Weapon System Programs* (prepared by the RAND Corporation for the United States Air Force, 2006), www.rand.org/pubs/ technical_reports/TR343.html; and Obaid Younossi and others, *Is Weapon System Cost Growth Increasing? A Quantitative Assessment of Completed and Ongoing Programs* (prepared by the RAND Corporation for the United States Air Force, 2007), www.rand.org/ pubs/monographs/MG588.html.

Figure 3-1.

Costs of DoD's Acquisition Plans

Billions of 2015 Dollars

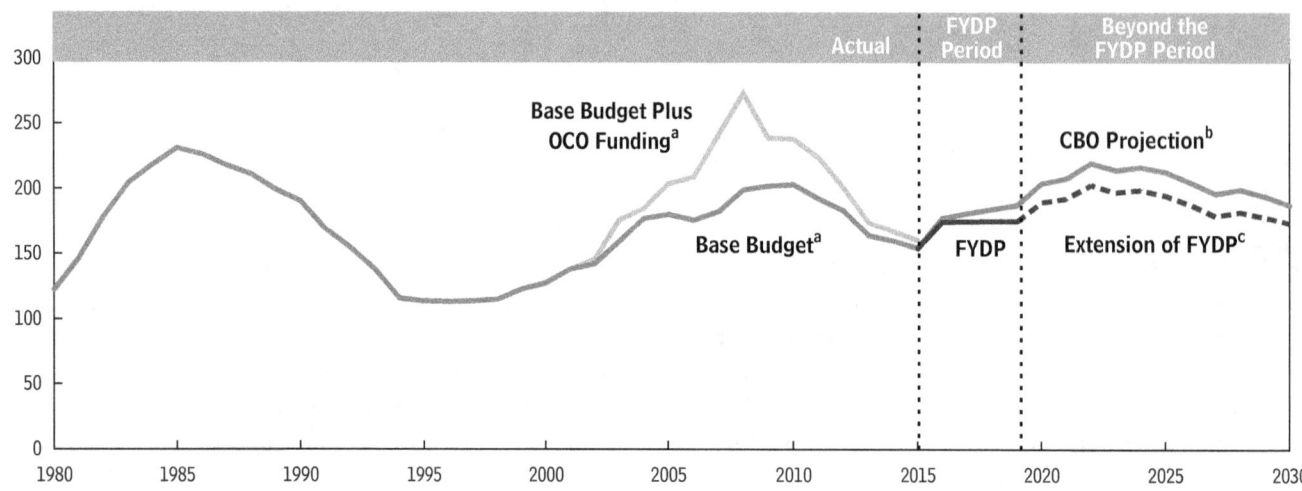

Source: Congressional Budget Office.

Note: DoD = Department of Defense; FYDP = Future Years Defense Program; OCO = overseas contingency operations; FYDP period = 2015 through 2019, the period for which DoD's plans are fully specified.

a.   Base-budget data include supplemental and emergency funding before 2002. For 2002 to 2015, supplemental and emergency funding for overseas contingency operations, such as those in Afghanistan and Iraq, and for other purposes is shown separately from the base-budget data. No OCO funding is shown for 2016 and later.

b.   The CBO projection of the base budget incorporates costs that are consistent with DoD's historical experience.

c.   For the extension of the FYDP from 2020 to 2030, CBO projects the costs of DoD's plans using the department's estimates of costs to the extent they are available and costs that are consistent with CBO's projections of price and compensation trends in the overall economy when the department's estimates are not available.

additional $10.7 billion in acquisition funding as part of the Administration's Opportunity, Growth, and Security Initiative, but that funding is not included in DoD's base-budget plans. This report does not address OCO or OGSI costs.

To project the costs of DoD's acquisition plans, CBO tracked the procurement and RDT&E funding for more than 190 weapon systems or major upgrades to existing systems (CBO refers to them as major systems). Some of those systems are in or nearing production (for example, the Air Force's KC-46 tanker), and some are in the early planning stages (for example, a new armored personnel carrier for the Army). Others (such as a replacement for the Navy's F/A-18E/F fighter) have no specific plans yet but have been identified by CBO either as systems that would be necessary to maintain weapon inventories when existing systems reach the end of their service life or as systems that would provide new capabilities to meet the goals described in the services' policy statements.

The following sections describe details of the most significant systems in DoD's acquisition plans and CBO's estimates of the costs of those plans for each of the military departments—the Army, the Navy (which includes the Marine Corps), and the Air Force—and for the parts of DoD outside of the military services, including the Missile Defense Agency, or MDA (see Figure 3-2).

The Army

The Department of the Army's 2015 request for acquisition funding includes $20 billion for the base budget. The Army also identified an additional $1.3 billion for acquisition for overseas contingency operations and $3.3 billion for acquisition as part of the OGSI. According to the CBO projection of DoD's plans, real acquisition costs for the Army's base budget would increase to $24 billion in 2016 (an increase of 18 percent) and then climb more slowly, reaching $26 billion at the end of the FYDP period (see Figure 3-3). In 2020, the first year after the FYDP period, real costs would rise again, to

Figure 3-2.

Costs of DoD's Acquisition Plans, by Military Service

Billions of 2015 Dollars

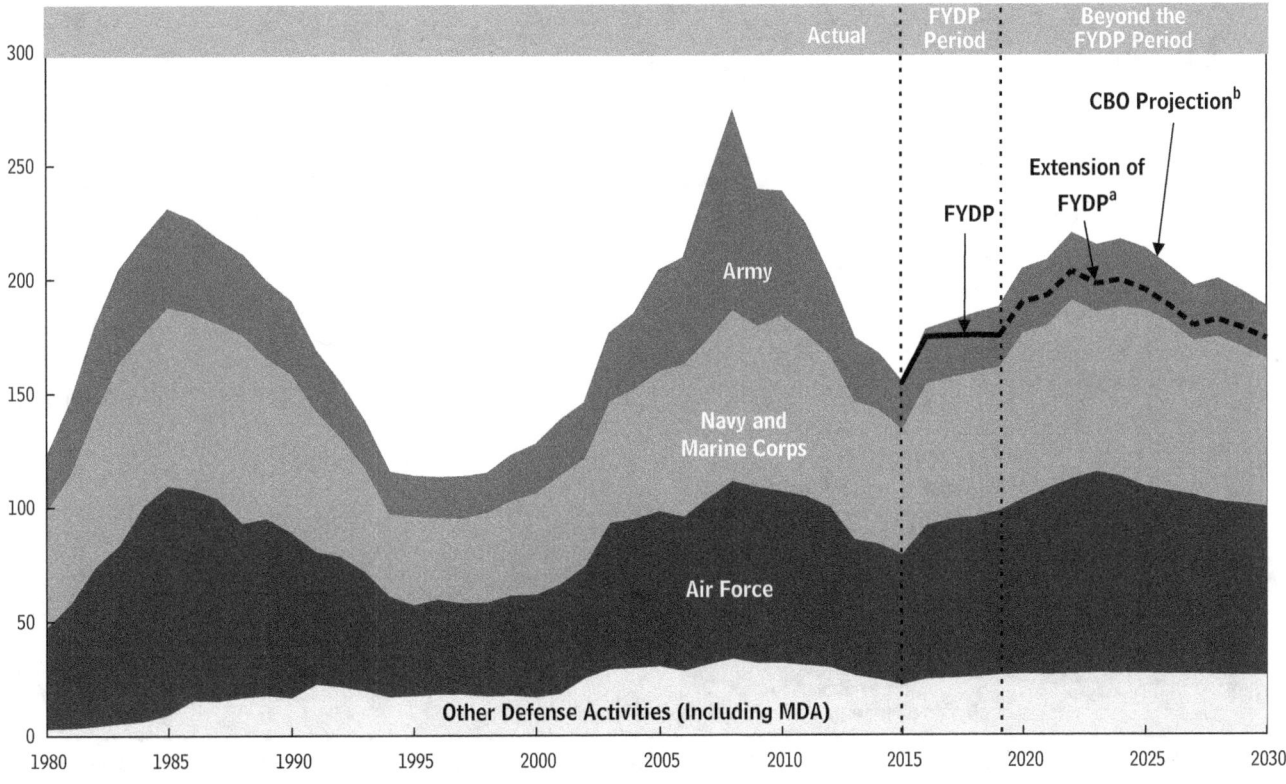

Source: Congressional Budget Office.

Notes: The amounts shown for the Future Years Defense Program (FYDP) and the extension of the FYDP are the totals for all categories.

  DoD = Department of Defense; FYDP period = 2015 through 2019, the period for which DoD's plans are fully specified;
  MDA = Missile Defense Agency.

a. For the extension of the FYDP from 2020 to 2030, CBO projects the costs of DoD's plans using the department's estimates of costs to the
    extent they are available and costs that are consistent with CBO's projections of price and compensation trends in the overall economy
    when the department's estimates are not available.

b. Each category shows total funding (including overseas contingency operations) for 1980 to 2014 and the CBO projection of the base
    budget from 2015 to 2030. That projection incorporates costs that are consistent with DoD's historical experience.

about $28 billion, and would remain at roughly that level through 2025 before declining thereafter. Real acquisition costs for the Army in the FYDP and extension have a similar profile, but total estimated costs for 2020 through 2030 are 13 percent lower than the costs estimated in the CBO projection.

For its projections of procurement costs for the Army, CBO tracked selected programs in five categories of major systems: ground combat vehicles and trucks; command, control, communications, computers, intelligence, surveillance, and reconnaissance (C4ISR) systems; aircraft; missiles and munitions; and missile defense

systems. Less costly vehicles (such as pickup trucks), weapons and munitions (such as small arms ammunition), and other items purchased with procurement appropriations are grouped together as "other procurement."[2] Funding for RDT&E is displayed as a separate category.

---

2. CBO's procurement categories do not directly correspond with
    the services' appropriation accounts. For example, CBO's category
    for Army aircraft includes only major programs contained in the
    broader "Aircraft Procurement, Army" appropriation account.
    Smaller programs in that account are included in CBO's other
    procurement category.

Figure 3-3.

Costs of the Army's Acquisition Plans

Billions of 2015 Dollars

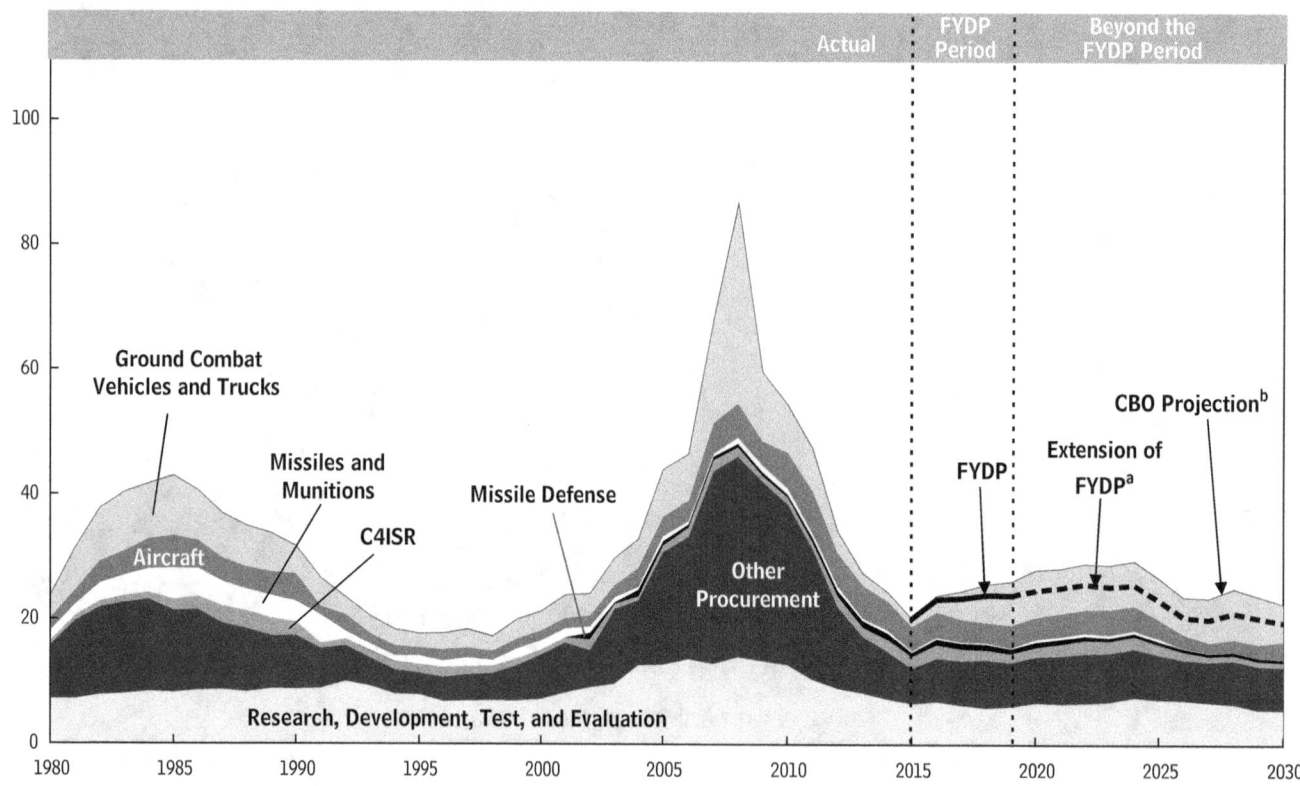

Source: Congressional Budget Office.

Notes: The amounts shown for the Future Years Defense Program (FYDP) and the extension of the FYDP are the totals for all categories.

FYDP period = 2015 through 2019, the period for which the Department of Defense's (DoD's) plans are fully specified; C4ISR = command, control, communications, computers, intelligence, surveillance, and reconnaissance.

a. For the extension of the FYDP from 2020 to 2030, CBO projects the costs of DoD's plans using the department's estimates of costs to the extent they are available and costs that are consistent with CBO's projections of price and compensation trends in the overall economy when the department's estimates are not available.

b. Each category shows total funding (including overseas contingency operations) for 1980 to 2014 and the CBO projection of the base budget from 2015 to 2030. That projection incorporates costs that are consistent with DoD's historical experience.

Ground Combat Vehicles and Trucks

The Army's plans include upgrades to some of its combat vehicles, such as Abrams tanks, Bradley fighting vehicles, and self-propelled 155-millimeter howitzers. The Army also plans to purchase a new combat vehicle, the armored multipurpose vehicle (AMPV), which would replace the various versions of the M113 armored personnel carrier in the Army's combat brigades. Procurement for AMPVs would begin in 2018. The Army canceled the Ground Combat Vehicle—its largest acquisition program—in late 2013, and it will instead continue to modify and enhance the current Bradley fighting vehicle. CBO assumed that

the Army would begin to procure replacements for the Bradley fighting vehicle in 2022 and the Abrams tank in 2027.

In addition to combat vehicles, the Army intends to modernize or upgrade some of its other tactical vehicles, which are primarily various types of trucks. The Army's plans include the purchase of a light truck that is being developed in cooperation with the Marine Corps. Called the Joint Light Tactical Vehicle (JLTV), it is expected to be better protected and more fuel-efficient than the Army's current light truck, the high-mobility multi-purpose wheeled vehicle (HMMWV, or "Humvee").

The Army plans to purchase about 29,000 JLTVs from 2015 through 2030, with the ultimate goal of replacing about one-third of the roughly 150,000 HMMWVs in its inventory with JLTVs. The Army will probably upgrade the HMMWVs that are not replaced. Costs for the Army's plans to extend the service life of its heavy and medium trucks are also included in CBO's projections.

C4ISR Systems

The Army's C4ISR systems include radios and other equipment that enable Army units to communicate and to share data. Two of the larger programs in that category are for new and more advanced radios that would provide increasingly sophisticated networking capabilities: the Joint Tactical Radio System (JTRS) and the Warfighter Information Network-Tactical (WIN-T) data-networking system. The Army intends to buy nearly 240,000 radios through two JTRS programs from 2015 through 2033, and it plans to purchase hardware and software through the WIN-T program in three increments through 2025.

Aircraft

The Army's plans for aviation programs include both manned and unmanned aircraft. Those plans include completing purchases of UH-72A Lakota light-utility helicopters, which are replacing the Army's remaining UH-1H Hueys and OH-58C Kiowas. The 2015 FYDP calls for 100 more Lakotas than previously planned; those additional aircraft are to be used to train pilots. The Army has abandoned near-term plans for purchasing armed scout helicopters to replace today's fleet of OH-58D Kiowa Warriors. Current plans call for retiring the OH-58D and using Apache attack helicopters and unmanned aircraft instead. The Army would develop and field a new aerial scout system in the 2020s, CBO assumes. The projections for Army aircraft also include development of a future vertical lift aircraft, production of which would begin in 2029. In addition, the projections include the Army's plans to upgrade and extend the service life of its Apache, Blackhawk, and Chinook helicopters. The projections also take into account plans to complete purchases of the MQ-1C Grey Eagle—an unmanned aircraft that is similar to the Predator flown by the Air Force—in 2015 and plans to purchase smaller unmanned aircraft.[3]

---

3. For related discussion, see Congressional Budget Office, *Policy Options for Unmanned Aircraft Systems* (June 2011), www.cbo.gov/publication/41448.

Missiles and Munitions

The Army plans to continue purchases of several types of missiles and munitions. Those include ongoing purchases of the Javelin missile that can be launched by individual soldiers. Planned purchases of artillery munitions include the Excalibur, a guided 155-millimeter cannon shell, and rockets for guided multiple-launch rocket systems.

Missile Defense

In recent years, the Army has planned to buy two systems to defend against ballistic missiles: the Patriot Air and Missile Defense System, which includes the Patriot Advanced Capability-3 (PAC-3) missile, and the Patriot/Medium Extended Air Defense System (MEADS) Combined Aggregate Program, which was intended to be a follow-on to the Patriot system. However, DoD chose to terminate the MEADS program after a development effort that ended in 2013. Current plans include procurement of the Patriot Missile Segment Enhancement interceptor, which is compatible with the Patriot system and is expected to perform better than the PAC-3 missile, in quantities similar to those anticipated in the MEADS program before it was terminated. The Army now plans to upgrade other components of its existing Patriot systems as well.

The Navy and the Marine Corps

The portion of the 2015 budget request covering the base budget for the Department of the Navy, which comprises the Navy and the Marine Corps, contains $55 billion for acquisition. The department also identified an additional $693 million for acquisition for overseas contingency operations and $3.3 billion for acquisition as part of the OGSI. According to the CBO projection of DoD's plans, real acquisition costs for the base budget of the Navy and the Marine Corps would rise to $62 billion in 2016—an increase of 13 percent in one year—and to $63 billion by the end of the FYDP period. Such costs would average $61 billion from 2015 through 2019, 3 percent higher than the average anticipated in the FYDP (see Figure 3-4).

Beyond the FYDP period, the real costs to implement the Navy's and Marine Corps' acquisition plans would, according to the CBO projection, increase substantially, jumping to $73 billion in 2020 (16 percent more than the 2019 amount) and averaging $72 billion per year

Figure 3-4.

Costs of the Navy's and Marine Corps' Acquisition Plans

Billions of 2015 Dollars

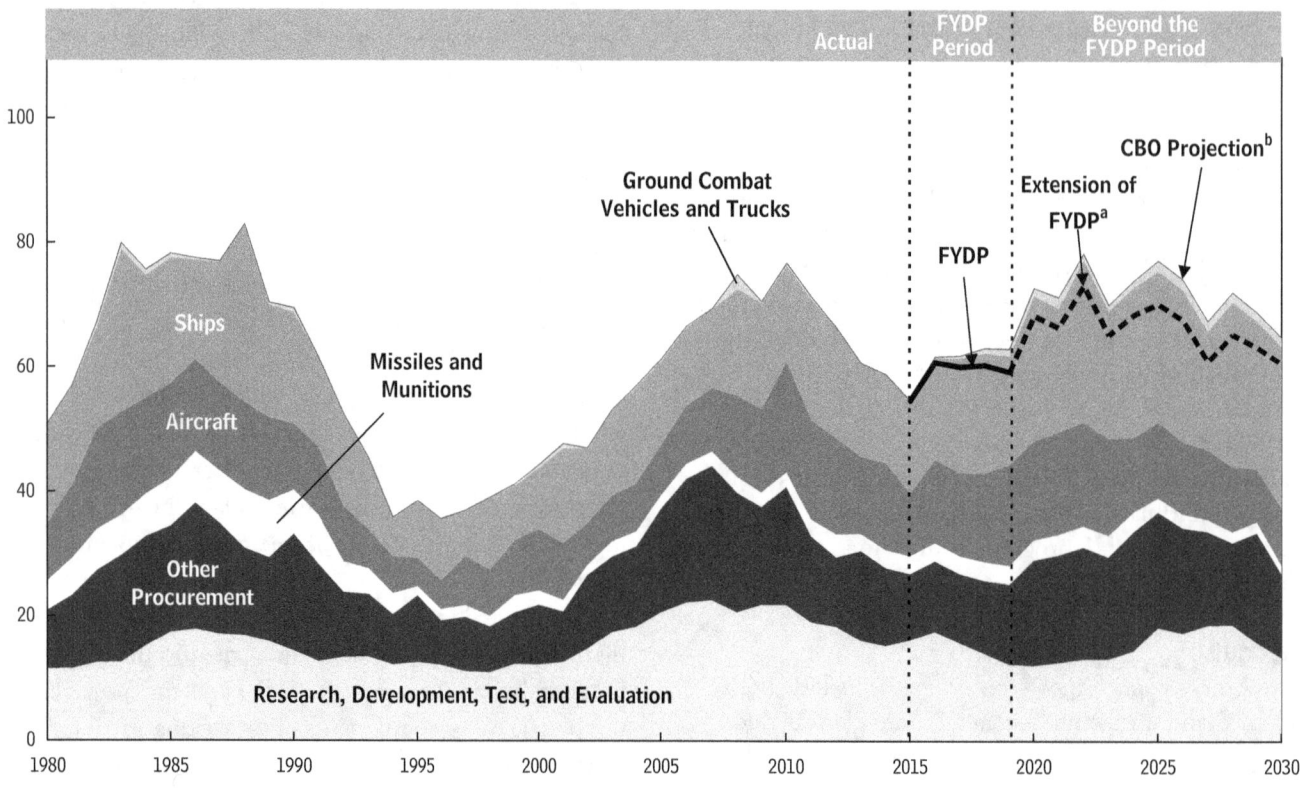

Source: Congressional Budget Office.

Notes: The amounts shown for the Future Years Defense Program (FYDP) and the extension of the FYDP are the totals for all categories.

FYDP period = 2015 through 2019, the period for which the Department of Defense's (DoD's) plans are fully specified.

a. For the extension of the FYDP from 2020 to 2030, CBO projects the costs of DoD's plans using the department's estimates of costs to the extent they are available and costs that are consistent with CBO's projections of price and compensation trends in the overall economy when the department's estimates are not available.

b. Each category shows total funding (including overseas contingency operations) for 1980 to 2014 and the CBO projection of the base budget from 2015 to 2030. That projection incorporates costs that are consistent with DoD's historical experience.

from 2020 through 2030. Real acquisition costs for the Navy and the Marine Corps in the FYDP and extension have a similar profile, but total estimated costs for 2020 through 2030 are 8 percent lower than the costs estimated under the CBO projection.

In analyzing procurement costs for the Navy and the Marine Corps, CBO tracked selected programs in four categories of major systems: ships, aircraft, ground combat vehicles and trucks for the Marine Corps, and missiles and munitions. Less costly weapon systems and munitions as well as other items purchased with procurement funding are grouped together as other procurement. As with the Army, funding for RDT&E is shown separately.

Ships

The Navy requested nearly $15 billion in 2015 for programs that fall into CBO's ship category. That total includes funding for ship construction and major modifications plus additional funding for mission modules purchased for littoral combat ships (LCSs). The Navy's fiscal year 2015 plans reflect the goal of expanding the fleet from today's 290 ships to 306 ships.[4] According to the CBO projection, those plans would cost an average of $22 billion per year between 2015 and 2030 in real terms; under the FYDP and extension, those costs would average about $1 billion per year less.

Surface Combatants. The Navy's surface combatant force consists of 95 cruisers, destroyers, and small surface combatants such as frigates (the last of which will be retired in 2015) and LCSs. The 2015 FYDP calls for purchasing 10 DDG-51 destroyers and 14 LCSs through 2019. For 2020 through 2030, CBO projects purchases of an additional 28 DDG-51s and 18 LCSs. The LCS quantities would result in a total of 52 small surface combatants, although the Navy has said that it may change the design of the LCS after the 32nd ship or build a new type of small ship instead. CBO's projection also includes the costs of extensive modernization and life extension of 11 Ticonderoga class cruisers.

Submarines. The Navy's submarine force consists of 54 attack submarines (SSNs), 4 guided missile submarines, and 14 ballistic missile submarines (SSBNs).[5] The 2015 FYDP calls for purchasing 10 Virginia class SSNs through 2019. For 2020 through 2030, CBO projects purchases of an additional one or two SSNs per year. The Navy also plans to replace today's fleet of Ohio-class SSBNs with 12 new ships by 2035. The first replacement SSBN would be purchased in 2021, followed by a second SSBN in 2024 and then one SSBN per year starting in 2026. The guided missile submarines would not be replaced when they reach the end of their service life.

Amphibious and Maritime Prepositioning Ships. The Navy's plans call for a force of 33 amphibious ships, including 11 large-deck amphibious assault ships. According to CBO's projections, the Navy would purchase 4 large-deck amphibious assault ships through 2033. The projections also incorporate purchases of replacements for the LSD-41 and LSD-49 dock landing ships beginning in 2020.[6]

---

4. CBO's projection of the FYDP and extension is, for Navy shipbuilding, based on the Navy's explicit 30-year shipbuilding plans and associated cost estimates. CBO's own projection is based on the same plans but with CBO's estimates of costs. For more details, see Congressional Budget Office, *An Analysis of the Navy's Fiscal Year 2015 Shipbuilding Plan* (forthcoming).

5. For additional discussion of ballistic missile submarines and their costs, see Congressional Budget Office, *Projected Costs of U.S. Nuclear Forces, 2014 to 2023* (December 2013), www.cbo.gov/publication/44968.

6. For related analysis, see Congressional Budget Office, *An Analysis of the Navy's Amphibious Warfare Ships for Deploying Marines Overseas* (November 2011), www.cbo.gov/publication/42716.

Aircraft Carriers. The Navy currently operates 10 large-deck, nuclear powered aircraft carriers (CVNs), but its longer-term plans call for 11 of those ships. Under the 2015 FYDP, the Navy would order a third Ford-class CVN in 2018. In CBO's projections, 3 more would follow by 2033, one every five years. In addition, the Navy plans to continue refueling and overhauling today's Nimitz class aircraft carriers, although the 2015 FYDP delays until 2016 a decision about funding the refueling and overhauling of the *George Washington*. Five Nimitz class ships have been or are in the process of being overhauled. CBO's projection takes into account the overhaul of 4 more Nimitz class ships planned through 2030 but does not include costs of the overhaul of the *George Washington*. (A decision to proceed with overhauling that carrier would add nearly $4 billion to shipbuilding costs over the next three years.)

Aircraft

The Department of the Navy's aviation programs include Navy and Marine Corps aircraft and aircraft-related weapon systems. For 2015, the Administration requested $9 billion to procure 103 new aircraft. The Navy and Marine Corps operate high-performance fighters, a wide variety of other fixed-wing aircraft (including long-range patrol aircraft, airlifters, and tankers), and helicopters and tilt-rotor aircraft designed for attack, reconnaissance, and transport of cargo and personnel. Annual real costs would rise steadily through 2022—from $10 billion in 2015 to nearly $17 billion in 2022—before declining thereafter.

Fighter Aircraft. The Navy did not request any more F/A-18E/F Super Hornet strike fighters or EA-18G Growler electronic warfare aircraft in the 2015 FYDP. Acquisition of fighter aircraft is now focused primarily on continuing development of the F-35 Joint Strike Fighter (both the F-35B short takeoff/vertical landing version and the F-35C carrier-based version). Under current schedules, 604 of those aircraft would be purchased between 2015 and the end of production in 2033, mostly to replace today's A through D model F/A-18 Hornets and AV-8B Harriers. The Navy is also expected to begin exploring alternatives for a new fighter to replace the F/A-18E/Fs, the oldest of which are expected to reach the end of their service lives in the late 2020s or early 2030s. Both the CBO projection and the FYDP and extension reflect CBO's assumption that the Navy will opt for a new fighter design to replace the F/A-18E/F. Projected costs for that new fighter within the projection period are primarily for research and development beginning in 2019; initial production is assumed to begin in 2030.[7]

Other Fixed-Wing Aircraft. In addition to fighters, the Navy plans to purchase several other types of carrier- and land-based fixed-wing aircraft. Purchases are slated to continue for the latest version of the carrier-based E-2 Hawkeye airborne early-warning aircraft and for the land-based P-8A Poseidon patrol aircraft, which is based on a Boeing 737 airframe and is replacing the P-3C Orion. CBO's projections also include the MQ-4 Triton (an unmanned maritime surveillance aircraft that is a modified version of the Air Force's Global Hawk high-altitude unmanned aerial vehicle), procurement of which is scheduled to begin in 2016, and an Unmanned Carrier-Launched Airborne Surveillance and Strike aircraft that would enter service early in the next decade.

Tilt-Rotor and Rotary-Wing Aircraft. The Navy's plans include procurement of MH-60R/S helicopters and MQ-8A Firescout unmanned helicopters. Purchases of the former would be completed in 2015; purchases of the latter, which have been suspended since 2011, would resume in 2020. CBO's projections also include a program to replace older MH-60 helicopters starting in the 2020s.

The Marine Corps' plans call for replacing or upgrading nearly every component of its tilt-rotor and rotary-wing forces. The Marine Corps is continuing to replace its CH-46E medium-lift helicopters with MV-22 Osprey tilt-rotor aircraft and is modernizing its fleets of UH-1N light-utility helicopters and AH-1W attack helicopters. The Marine Corps is also developing a new heavy-lift helicopter—the CH-53K—to replace today's fleet of heavy-lift CH-53E helicopters. In addition, development is under way for a replacement for the current Marine One Presidential transport helicopters.

Ground Combat Vehicles and Trucks

In its projection for ground combat vehicles, CBO assumed that the Marine Corps would continue with its plan to develop a new amphibious combat vehicle to replace the amphibious assault vehicle that is in use today. In the short term, the plan involves extending the service life of existing amphibious assault vehicles. In the longer

term, the Marine Corps would develop and purchase a new amphibious combat vehicle, but the capabilities, quantities, and program schedule for that system have not yet been finalized. Under the CBO projection, procurement of that vehicle would begin in 2021 and continue beyond the projection period. CBO's projections also include funds to procure 5,500 JLTVs that are being developed with the Army. The JLTVs for the Marine Corps would be purchased from 2015 through 2022.

Missiles and Munitions

Missiles and munitions encompass air-launched weapons (air-to-air and air-to-ground missiles) and ship-launched weapons (defensive surface-to-air missiles, antiship missiles, land-attack missiles, and torpedoes). Notable among the Department of the Navy's plans for those weapons are purchases of a substantial number of Standard missiles for fleet air defense, a new missile for attacking surface ships, torpedoes for attacking surface ships and submarines, and air-launched Joint Standoff Weapons for attacking ground targets.

The Air Force

The Department of the Air Force's 2015 request for acquisition funding in its base budget is $57 billion. The Air Force also identified an additional $3.8 billion for acquisition for overseas contingency operations and $3.5 billion for acquisition as part of the OGSI. According to the CBO projection of DoD's plans, the Air Force's real acquisition costs for its base budget would increase by 18 percent between 2015 and 2016 and by 26 percent over the entire period of the FYDP, to $72 billion in 2019 (see Figure 3-5). Total costs anticipated in the FYDP for 2015 through 2019 are 4 percent lower than under the CBO projection.

Beyond the FYDP period, real costs for the Air Force's acquisition plans would, under the CBO projection, increase steadily to $88 billion in 2023 and then average $80 billion per year through the end of the projection period. Real acquisition costs for the Air Force in the FYDP and extension follow a similar pattern, but they average 8 percent less than in the CBO projection.

For its projections of procurement costs for the Air Force, CBO tracked selected programs in three categories of major systems: aircraft, missiles and munitions, and space systems. Less costly weapon systems and munitions as well

---

7. Instead of developing a new aircraft, the Navy might opt to purchase additional F-35Cs. That course of action would result in lower RDT&E costs than are reflected in CBO's analysis.

Figure 3-5.

Costs of the Air Force's Acquisition Plans

Billions of 2015 Dollars

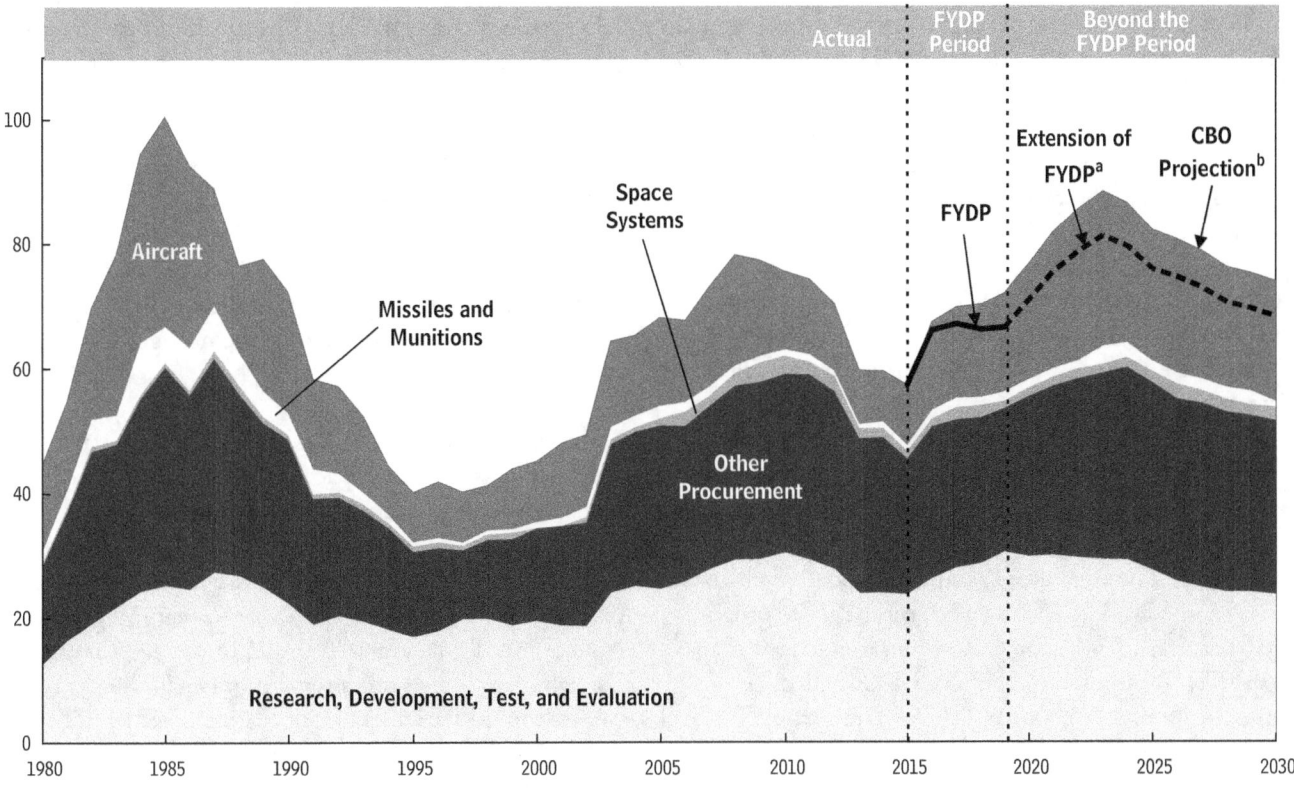

Source: Congressional Budget Office.

Notes: The amounts shown for the Future Years Defense Program (FYDP) and the extension of the FYDP are the totals for all categories.

FYDP period = 2015 through 2019, the period for which the Department of Defense's (DoD's) plans are fully specified.

a.   For the extension of the FYDP from 2020 to 2030, CBO projects the costs of DoD's plans using the department's estimates of costs to the extent they are available and costs that are consistent with CBO's projections of price and compensation trends in the overall economy when the department's estimates are not available.

b.   Each category shows total funding (including overseas contingency operations) for 1980 to 2014 and the CBO projection of the base budget from 2015 to 2030. That projection incorporates costs that are consistent with DoD's historical experience.

as other purchases made with procurement funding are grouped together as "other procurement." Funding for RDT&E is also assigned to a separate category.

Aircraft

The Air Force's plans include purchases of new aircraft and major modifications to existing aircraft. According to the CBO projection, the costs in the aircraft category would rise significantly, from $9.5 billion in 2015 to nearly $16 billion in 2019 and $25 billion in 2023. After 2023, the costs to procure new aircraft would decline slowly through the end of the projection period. The number of aircraft purchased annually would increase substantially, from 58 in 2015 to more than 150 in 2023.

The Air Force's acquisition plans include several new aircraft that have not yet entered service.

F-35A Joint Strike Fighter. The Air Force is continuing with the development and initial production of the F-35A. Current plans call for procuring 26 F-35As in 2015 and increasing annual procurement to 80 aircraft by 2021. A total of 1,098 of those fighters would be purchased from 2015 to 2030, and production would continue through 2038.

KC-46A Airborne Tanker. The KC-46A is being developed by the Air Force to replace its fleet of KC-135 airborne tankers. Procurement is scheduled to begin with

7 aircraft in 2015, ramp up to 15 aircraft per year for 2019 through 2026, and end with 6 aircraft in 2027; the expected total would be 179 KC-46As. The Air Force has stated, however, that replacing its entire KC-135 fleet would require additional purchases beyond those planned for the KC-46A. For 2027 through 2030, therefore, CBO assumed that the Air Force would continue to purchase 15 tankers per year at costs similar to those for the KC-46A. The Air Force could, however, choose to develop a different type of aircraft (sometimes referred to as the KC-Y).

Combat Rescue Helicopter. The Air Force is implementing plans to replace its fleet of HH-60G Blackhawk Combat Search and Rescue (CSAR) helicopters with new aircraft based on an existing design. No funding for a CSAR replacement was included in the Administration's request for 2015, but the development would resume later in the FYDP, effectively deferring the CSAR replacement program by several years relative to the previous year's plans. The Air Force has since indicated plans to restore some funding in the near term to reduce or eliminate that delay. Under the CBO projection for the plans in the FYDP, production of a new CSAR helicopter would begin in 2020, and 112 such aircraft would be purchased over nine years.

Long-Range Strike Bomber. The Air Force is currently reviewing performance goals and available technologies in anticipation of developing a new long-range bomber to be fielded sometime after 2020. The 2015 FYDP posits steadily increasing annual funding for development of that system; CBO's analysis reflects the assumptions that development efforts would continue beyond the FYDP period and that procurement of the aircraft would begin in 2020.

T-X Trainer. The Air Force is currently working on defining a program to develop a new aircraft for advanced pilot training. This aircraft would replace the T-38 trainer that is in service today. CBO's projections include procurement of such an aircraft beginning in 2020.

Missiles and Munitions

The Air Force's missiles and munitions include systems that range from air-to-air weapons to intercontinental ballistic missiles (ICBMs). Plans include upgrades to existing Minuteman III ICBMs to keep them in service until at least 2030. Air-to-surface weapons include the Joint Air-to-Surface Standoff Missile, the Joint Direct Attack Munition, and the Small-Diameter Bomb. There are also plans to field a replacement for today's Air-Launched Cruise Missile that carries a nuclear warhead, although those plans are now delayed by three years relative to last year's FYDP. Under the CBO projection, procurement of those missiles would begin in 2026.

Space Systems

Space systems consist mainly of satellites and the launch systems used to put them into orbit. In its proposed budget for 2015, the Air Force has continued acquisition initiatives that it began in the 2012 budget for the current generation of satellites, and it has been examining a variety of approaches for fielding the next generation of satellites.

For current-generation satellite programs, the strategy (referred to as Efficient Space Procurement) features blocks of satellites purchased at fixed prices ("block buys") combined with ongoing technology development for follow-on systems. Procurement budgets for those programs would vary less from year to year by spreading costs over multiple years. In the 2015 budget, the Air Force has continued procurement of (small) blocks of two Advanced Extremely High Frequency Satellites and two Space-Based Infrared System satellites.

The Air Force is considering several approaches for fielding the next generation of satellites, including separating functions that had been carried on a single satellite onto several smaller satellites (a practice referred to as disaggregation) and hosting DoD payloads on commercial satellites. Those approaches are intended to improve the resiliency of U.S. space assets against potential attack by antisatellite weapons. The approaches are also hoped to reduce the cost of space systems, but the effect on costs is not yet known.

The Air Force has also continued its efforts to improve efficiency in the procurement of the Evolved Expendable Launch Vehicle (EELV) for launching satellites. In December 2013, the Air Force completed a new contract that includes block buys of EELVs, with the goal of reducing cost by providing a more stable demand for the vehicles. In addition, the Air Force plans to increase competition for EELV acquisition by certifying new firms to provide launch services. However, the service reduced the number of launches that will be open to competition between 2015 and 2017; last year's plan called for 14, but the current plan includes only 7.

Figure 3-6.

Costs of DoD's Acquisition Plans Other Than Those for the Military Services

Billions of 2015 Dollars

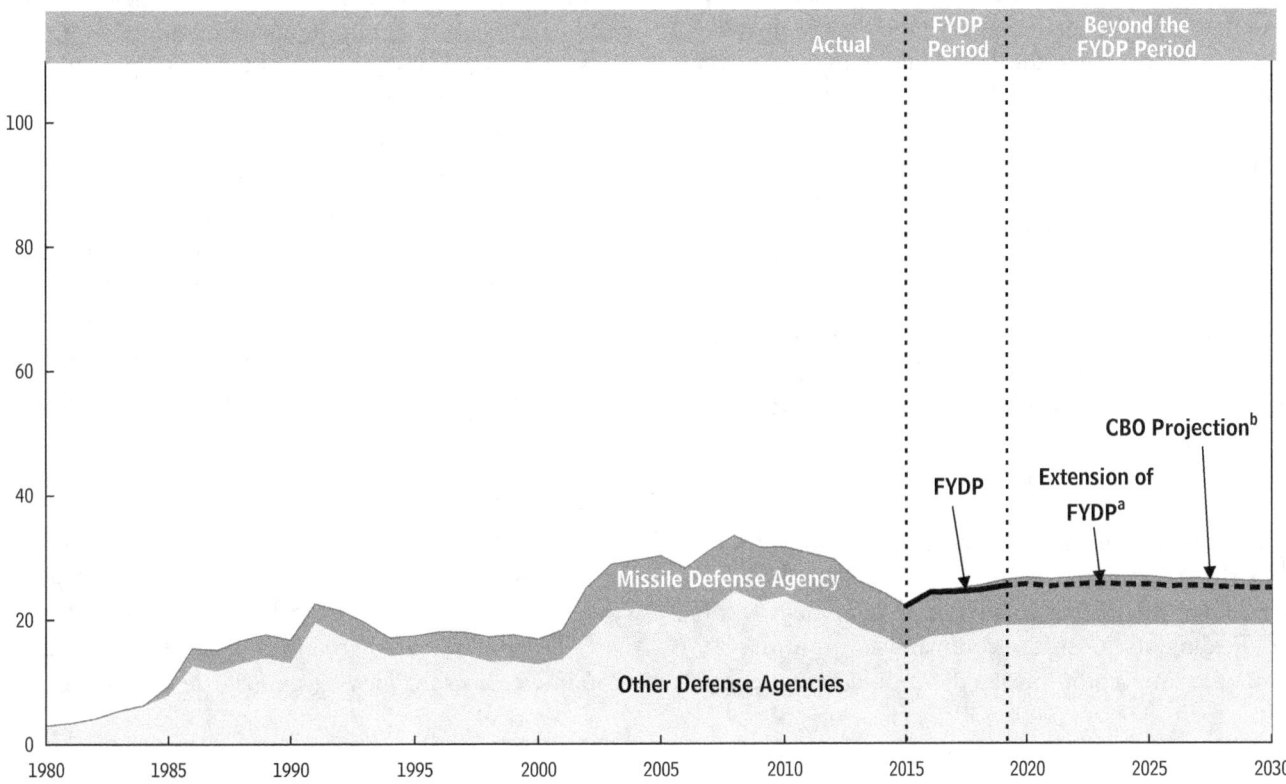

Source: Congressional Budget Office.

Notes: The amounts shown for the Future Years Defense Program (FYDP) and the extension of the FYDP are the totals for all categories.

   DoD = Department of Defense; FYDP period = 2015 through 2019, the period for which DoD's plans are fully specified.

a.   For the extension of the FYDP from 2020 to 2030, CBO projects the costs of DoD's plans using the department's estimates of costs to the extent they are available and costs that are consistent with CBO's projections of price and compensation trends in the overall economy when the department's estimates are not available.

b.   Each category shows total funding (including overseas contingency operations) for 1980 to 2014 and the CBO projection of the base budget from 2015 to 2030. That projection incorporates costs that are consistent with DoD's historical experience.

Other Defense Activities, Including Those of the Missile Defense Agency

In addition to funding for acquisition by the Departments of the Army, Navy, and Air Force, DoD's budget includes funding for acquisition by its other components, including specialized agencies that perform advanced research, develop missile defenses, oversee special operations, and manage financial and information systems. For the 2015 base budget, DoD requested $22 billion for acquisition related to those activities. DoD also identified $279 million for such acquisition in its OCO request for 2015 and $517 million for acquisition in 2015 as part of

the OGSI, but those amounts are not part of DoD's base budget and are not included in this analysis. According to the CBO projection, the base-budget costs of acquisition for the other components of DoD would increase to more than $24 billion in 2016 and rise to more than $26 billion in the final year of the FYDP period. Beyond the FYDP period, CBO assumed that real acquisition costs for defense organizations other than the Missile Defense Agency would remain constant at $19 billion— the amount indicated in the FYDP for 2019 (see Figure 3-6); it estimated costs for MDA on a programmatic basis.

The 2015 budget request for MDA was $7.0 billion for acquisition ($5.6 billion for RDT&E and $1.4 billion for procurement), about $400 million for operation and maintenance, and about $40 million for military construction. This section deals only with the acquisition portion of the budget; the O&M and military construction portions are included in the analysis of those accounts in Chapters 2 and 4.

Over the 2015–2019 period, the real costs of MDA's plans for acquisition total about $36 billion under the CBO projection, including $28 billion for RDT&E and $8 billion for procurement. The amount of funding for acquisition called for in the FYDP is about 10 percent less. From 2015 through 2030, MDA's real acquisition costs would average $7.4 billion per year under the CBO projection. The total planned MDA budget in the 2015 FYDP is very similar to that in the 2014 FYDP.

MDA's mission spans the full development cycle for missile defense, from research on emerging technology for future weapon systems through the development, testing, and fielding of the sensors, command and control systems, and interceptor missiles that would engage enemy missiles. MDA plans to emphasize improvements in defense of the U.S. homeland through several changes to the Ground-Based Midcourse Defense (GMD) system and its supporting sensors. Those changes include developing and fielding a Long-Range Discrimination Radar to improve sensor coverage and resolution in the Pacific theater, redesigning the Exoatmospheric Kill Vehicle for GMD interceptors with the goal of improving performance and reliability, and making several other improvements to the overall system intended to increase the ability to discriminate true targets from other objects that may surround them (such as decoys or debris from the rockets that launched the targets). The increased budget for GMD and its sensors in the 2015 FYDP is partially offset by a delay in the planned ramp-up in purchases of the SM-3 IB variant of interceptors for the Aegis missile defense system as that interceptor completes development and enters production. That delay notwithstanding, procurement funding from 2015 through 2019 would cover the purchase of more than 400 interceptors—157 interceptors for the Terminal High-Altitude Area Defense system, 8 ground-based interceptors, and 256 interceptors for the Aegis missile defense system.

Projections of Military Construction and Family Housing Costs

The military construction and family housing budgets that support the infrastructure of military installations together make up a small fraction of the Department of Defense's costs. In the 2015 budget, the request for military construction was $5.4 billion and the request for family housing was $1.2 billion—only 1.1 percent and 0.2 percent, respectively, of DoD's total base-budget request. The Administration also included $3 billion in funding for military construction and $80 million for family housing in its Opportunity, Growth, and Security Initiative proposal; the Congressional Budget Office did not treat that funding as part of DoD's base-budget request.

Military Construction

Appropriations for military construction pay for the planning, design, construction, and major restoration of military facilities. Those appropriations also pay for the base realignment and closure (BRAC) process, including environmental assessments of sites designated for closure and construction projects needed to help consolidate personnel and units.

Excluding funding for BRAC, DoD's plans call for $5.1 billion in funding for military construction in 2015, $7.3 billion in 2016, and an average of $5.9 billion in the final three years of the Future Years Defense Program period. Those amounts are significantly below the $8 billion in funding for military construction that DoD received, on average, from 1980 to 2014, excluding funding for overseas contingency operations and BRAC. Because infrastructure degrades slowly, DoD's plans under the current budget constraints prioritize funding for training and readiness over funding for military construction.[1] Indeed, DoD states that its request for the military construction budget is not sufficient to prevent long-term deterioration of its facilities.[2] (The OGSI proposal would help mitigate that shortfall in 2015 by adding $3 billion for military construction.) Under the extension of the FYDP, CBO based its estimates on historical average amounts of funding for construction. Real (inflation-adjusted) costs are projected to be $8 billion in 2020 and to grow steadily to about $9 billion in 2030, because the cost of construction is projected to rise at a slightly faster rate than economywide inflation.

Under the CBO projection, DoD's military construction costs excluding BRAC would rise from $5.1 billion in 2015 to about $10 billion in 2016 and remain at that level through 2019. CBO's projection is based on funding that is consistent with renovating or replacing facilities every 67 years, on average—a benchmark traditionally used by DoD.[3] Lower levels of funding could

---

1. Testimony of John Conger, Acting Deputy Under Secretary of Defense for Installations and Environment, before the Subcommittee on Military Construction, Veterans Affairs, and Related Agencies of the House Appropriations Committee (March 12, 2014), www.acq.osd.mil/ie/ie_library.shtml#test.

2. Department of Defense, *Fiscal Year 2015 Budget Request: Overview* (March 2014), p. 1-5, http://go.usa.gov/vP59 (PDF, 2.43 MB).

3. DoD recently moved away from the 67-year service life as a benchmark and now uses a model to more precisely estimate its recapitalization requirement from the bottom up. CBO, however, does not have access to that model and continues to use a 67-year service life as the basis for its projections. Excluding buildings used for family housing, DoD estimates that the current replacement value for all of its buildings, structures, and linear structures (such as roads and pipelines) is about $800 billion. Recapitalizing one-sixty-seventh of DoD's facilities each year would cost between $11 billion and $12 billion, 90 percent of which CBO estimates would be paid out of the military construction budget, with the remainder covered by restoration and modernization activities within the operation and maintenance budget.

force DoD to reduce the number of its facilities or to continue using facilities beyond their expected service lives. After the FYDP period, the CBO projection incorporates the assumption that funding for military construction would be sufficient to continue to meet the 67-year recapitalization benchmark. Therefore, real costs are projected to grow from $10 billion in 2020 to $11 billion in 2030.

DoD's military construction plans also include expenditures associated with past and potential future rounds of BRAC. Between 2015 and 2019, DoD's plans call for an average of about $300 million annually to cover ongoing environmental and caretaking costs for properties that were closed through the BRAC process in previous years and have not been converted to other uses. Under both the CBO projection and FYDP and extension, those costs would remain constant (in real terms) at about $300 million per year after 2019.

In addition, DoD's plans include more than $2 billion in total funding from 2016 through 2019 for a future round of BRAC that would commence in 2017. In the FYDP and extension, CBO assumes that any savings resulting from a future round of BRAC would not reduce the total DoD budget; rather, DoD is assumed to use those savings as a source of additional operation and maintenance funding for other purposes. The CBO projection incorporates the assumption that the Congress will

oppose further rounds of base closure and therefore that no extra funding would be required and no extra savings would be realized.

Family Housing

Appropriations for family housing pay for the construction, operation, maintenance, and leasing of military family housing. Those appropriations also support DoD's Homeowners Assistance Fund, which, under certain circumstances, compensates eligible military and civilian personnel who suffer financial loss from the sale of their primary residence. Appropriations for family housing have fallen sharply since 2007 because, under a DoD program to have private companies build and maintain housing on bases, funding for construction and operations of most housing units comes primarily from private financing that is not recorded in the federal budget. As a result, under both the CBO projection and the FYDP and extension, real appropriations for family housing are projected to remain at $1.3 billion—the amount that DoD projects in 2019—through 2030. Although the private financing reduces DoD's costs for building and operating family housing, it increases the government's costs for the basic allowance for housing that military personnel receive to rent those private housing units. Those housing allowances appear in military personnel costs in the operation and support budget.

List of Tables and Figures

Tables

Figures

About This Document

This Congressional Budget Office report was prepared at the request of the Chairman and Ranking Member of the Senate Committee on the Budget. In keeping with CBO's mandate to provide objective, impartial analysis, the report makes no recommendations.

David Arthur and Daniel Frisk of CBO's National Security Division coordinated the preparation of the report with guidance from David E. Mosher and Matthew S. Goldberg. Elizabeth Bass, Michael Bennett, Bernard Kempinski, Eric J. Labs, and Adam Talaber of the National Security Division contributed to the analysis. Kent Christensen, Raymond Hall, David Newman, Dawn Sauter Regan, Matthew Schmit, and Jason Wheelock of the Defense, International Affairs, and Veterans' Affairs Cost Estimates Unit in the Budget Analysis Division, with guidance from Sarah Jennings, also contributed to the report. Adebayo Adedeji fact-checked the manuscript.

Jeffrey Kling and Robert Sunshine reviewed the report, and Jeanine Rees edited and prepared it for publication. An electronic version is available on CBO's Web site (www.cbo.gov/publication/49483).

Douglas W. Elmendorf
Director

November 2014